Literature Discussion Groups in the Intermediate Grades

Dilemmas and Possibilities

Karen S. Evans
Marquette University
Milwaukee, Wisconsin, USA

INTERNATIONAL
Reading
Association

800 Barksdale Road, PO Box 8139
Newark, Delaware 19714-8139, USA
www.reading.org

The International Reading Association attempts, through its publications, to provide a forum for a wide spectrum of opinions on reading. This policy permits divergent viewpoints without implying the endorsement of the Association.

Director of Publications   Joan M. Irwin
Editorial Director, Books and Special Projects   Matthew W. Baker
Special Projects Editor   Tori Mello Bachman
Permissions Editor   Janet S. Parrack
Associate Editor   Jeanine K. McGann
Production Editor   Shannon Benner
Editorial Assistant   Tyanna Collins
Publications Manager   Beth Doughty
Production Department Manager   Iona Sauscermen
Art Director   Boni Nash
Supervisor, Electronic Publishing   Anette Schütz-Ruff
Senior Electronic Publishing Specialist   Cheryl J. Strum
Electronic Publishing Specialist   Lynn Harrison
Proofreader   Charlene M. Nichols

Project Editor   Jeanine K. McGann

Cover Photo   Image Productions

Library of Congress Cataloging-in-Publication Data
Evans, Karen S.
    Literature discussion groups in the intermediate grades: dilemmas and possibilities/Karen S. Evans.
      p.   cm.--(Kids InSight series)
Includes bibliographical references and indexes.
    ISBN 0-87207-293-2
    1. Literature—Study and teaching (Elementary)   2. Reading (Elementary)
3. Children—Books and reading.   I. Title.   II. Series.
LB1575.E83   2001
372.64'044—dc21
2001000074

Printed in Canada

For Jerry and Claire

Contents

Note From the Series Editor   vii

Chapter 1

Literature Discussion Groups: An Introduction   1

Chapter 2

Why Should I Use Literature Discussion Groups,   19
and How Do I Implement Them in My Classroom?

Chapter 3

Avoiding Round-Robin Discussions: The Need   37
for Instructional Scaffolding

Chapter 4

Integrating Skills Instruction With   66
Literature Discussions

Chapter 5

Assessing Literature Discussion Groups   88

Chapter 6

Social and Cultural Influences   114
on Literature Discussions

Appendix A

List of Discussion Topics   137

Appendix B

Story Map with Character Perspectives Sheet   138

Appendix C

Student Self- and Peer-Assessment Form   139

Appendix D

Observation Grid   140

References   141

Children's and Young Adult Literature References   145

Index   147

Note From the Series Editor

It is a pleasure to introduce readers to Karen Evans and the fifth-grade students that she describes in her book. Karen shares stories from three different classrooms where students (with guidance from their teachers) participate in literature group discussions. She shares stories about discussions that work and those that are problematic to highlight the realities behind implementing this worthwhile yet complex way of engaging readers with texts. Karen's own multiethnic, urban classroom from Tucson, Arizona is featured in the book as well as another classroom from the same city. Racine, Wisconsin provides the setting for the third classroom, which is comprised of working-class kids and their teacher, Marcy. I am pleased that Karen's book has been selected by a respected panel of literacy experts to be published in the Kids InSight (KI) Series; I believe her book makes a tremendous contribution to the field of intermediate-grade elementary students' literacy.

The KI series provides practical information for K–12 teachers and brings to the fore the voices of children and adolescents as the basis for instructional decisions. Books in the series are designed to encourage educators to address the challenge of meeting the literacy needs of all students as individuals and learners in and out of our classrooms, while recognizing that there are no easy answers or quick fixes to achieving this goal. Sociocultural perspectives of how students learn are the foundation of each KI book, and the authors address learners' emotional, affective, and cognitive development. Dialoguing with other professionals, reading research findings in literacy and education, inquiring into teaching and learning processes, observing as well as talking and listening to students, documenting successful practices, and reflecting on literacy events using writing and analysis are strategies and actions embraced by the teachers described in KI books. The authors of these books allow us to see into their classrooms, or view their students' lives outside of school, so that we may learn about the thoughts and dreams of young people and the goals and planning processes of teachers. We are privy to how events actually unfold during formal and informal lessons—the successful and the less-than-successful moments—through the use of transcripts and interview comments woven throughout KI books.

In *Literature Discussion Groups in the Intermediate Grades: Dilemmas and Possibilities*, Karen Evans shares how she worked to keep kids *in sight* as she observed and wrote about students as they worked together in small-group discussions. Karen illustrates for us the power of helping kids learn to talk about books. Specifically, she shows us discussions where students seek to understand events from multiple characters' perspectives. She provides ideas about how to lead students to this level of talk and how to support them as they participate in discussions where they explore their own lives and what they might do in a particular character's position.

Throughout the text Karen reminds us that the selection of books is critical to the process of high-quality discussions, arming us with lists that evoke excitement in students such as Jessie, who related, "I hope I get to read *Sharing Susan* next time. I'm dying to read that book!" (p. 30). Karen analyzes for us what happens when teachers select tools for students to use, such as response logs, that we think may be helpful to students' learning and involvement in books, but that they see as boring busy work. In interviews with the students, Karen helps us glean additional *insights* about what literature discussions mean to learners. For example, as Risa noted, "I think it helps me because sometimes when I read I get lost and I just keep on reading and then after I stop [and discuss], it helps me to remember what happened" (p. 23).

In this book, Karen allows the learners to show us what they understand, what they feel, and how they use the knowledge and ideas gleaned from reading books that they connect to as intermediate-grade students. One of the most powerful techniques that Karen challenges us to use is one she learned from the work of Vivian Paley, who suggests that, at first, students' group work efforts may not seem substantive. Paley urges teachers to look again, keeping in mind how learners—with their unique backgrounds and interests—might view the events about which they read. Karen takes us inside this reanalysis process and shows us what can be learned by refocusing our view to encompass students' perspectives. By reconsidering our ideas about literacy learning and teaching, we find that literature discussions are opportunities for students to learn how to read, write, and think about literature, as well as places to learn about themselves and their peers. Karen Evans's clearly written text takes us on a journey into three classrooms where we discover what literature discussions groups can and cannot do to support literacy learning, how to use them effectively in our classrooms, and how to develop insights about intermediate-grade learners.

Deborah R. Dillon
Series Editor
Purdue University
West Lafayette, Indiana, USA

Kids InSight Review Board

Jan Turbill
University of Wollongong
Wollongong, New South Wales,
    Australia

Angela Ward
University of Saskatchewan
Saskatoon, Saskatchewan,
    Canada

Deborah A. Wooten
Glenwood Landing School
Glen Head, New York, USA

Josephine P. Young
Arizona State University
Tempe, Arizona, USA

Literature Discussion Groups: An Introduction

Early in the school year, a group of fifth-grade girls discusses the book Shiloh *(Naylor, 1991). Keely asks her groupmates if they can relate to Murty (the main character) in any way. The floodgates open and the girls begin to share wonderful stories about their pets and their pain over losing pets or watching them be mistreated.*

Kaitlyn: My dad is really nice but, um, one time he kicked our dog in the stomach.

Hannah: We have somebody living with us and he always tries to kick our dog and stuff and one time he hit my dog like this (gestures) and my dog went like this (gestures again), and she stayed like that for a whole week. And my dog's always nice to him. My dog wakes him up.

Keely: We had to give our dog to the Humane Society when we, um, moved into an apartment. I...I really miss her. She was, had been, my Christmas present. I couldn't believe it when my parents surprised me with a puppy. It was like the best. I was so excited! My dad wanted to call the Humane Society to see if anyone, to see if she had been adopted and find out who adopted her so we could like go visit her.

Hannah: We had to give our dog away just because our crummy old neighbor complained about him barking too much. I mean, he barked and all but he didn't bark that much. And, this is kinda embarrassing, but, the first day he left I cried (comforting sounds from other girls in group).

Keely: I know, I miss my dog too.

Kaitlyn: I have this neighbor who, her dog got cancer and had these
like big gross tumors that burst (exclaims of "gross!" from
other girls). I know it's gross (laughs but is immediately
sober again), but she eventually died after being sick for a
really long time. I was so sad about it that I almost cried.

The girls return to these ideas the next day when they discuss
whether Marty should return Shiloh to his abusive owner, Mr. Judd. The
girls are adamant that Mr. Judd should not be allowed to have Shiloh
back, and they use their experiences to support their opinions.

During another discussion group at the end of the school year, a
group of boys are fidgeting, mumbling, and telling each other to cooperate
or to say something. But no one has anything to say. Hidalgo laughs and
fiddles around. Finally Stefan says in a frustrated voice, "Come on Hidalgo, man, read your journal or something!" No response. They fiddle with
the microphone and Jalil gets upset about them touching it. Another long
pause ensues—the boys fidget, tap the table, and lean back in their chairs.
Again Stefan says in a frustrated voice, "Can we get on with the session?
Brad, you never asked no questions." Brad and Hidalgo start to accuse
each other of not doing anything, each claiming he has done something in
the discussion and each justifying what he has done. It is obvious that
they are frustrated and angry with each other. The boys know they are not
doing what they are supposed to be doing, but it seems that they just do
not know what to do to make it any better. They start grabbing each other's
literature journals and reading them; some silently, some aloud. This is
painful to watch. You can almost feel the frustration and sense of helplessness that stems from not knowing what to do to make their discussion
work better. Another pause occurs and they sit there looking at each other,
fidgeting, and mumbling. They start making singing noises.

These two vignettes, taken from the same fifth-grade classroom, illustrate the two main themes of this book: The possibilities and
dilemmas of using literature discussion groups in upper elementary
grade classrooms. When I listened to the girls in the *Shiloh* group, I was

reminded again of the possibilities that exist for our students as they engage in literature discussions. These girls were able to use experiences in their own lives to explore the book in ways that were personally meaningful. Through sharing personal stories of their pets, they were able to develop a richer connection to the characters in the story and, consequently, they created a deeper understanding of the themes and issues raised in the book. This vignette shows a snapshot of how book discussions have the potential to touch a personal chord with our students, to hook them into the story and the characters' lives, and hopefully, to help them become lifelong readers. It is this type of discussion, one that I have observed countless times during my years of work with literature groups, that convinces me that literature discussions are a positive aspect of literacy programs.

The second small-group discussion with Hidalgo and his peers reveals the possible dilemmas and frustrations that exist for teachers trying to use literature discussions in classrooms. I wrote the journal entry in the vignette after observing a group of boys who were reading the novel *Scorpions* (Myers, 1988). To say I was disheartened by what I saw would be an understatement. Here was a situation where all the recommended factors were in place for a fabulous literature discussion, yet the types of meaningful discussions that were possible never became a reality. These students had been participating in literature discussion groups for an entire school year at this point. They were all reading their first choice of literature books, *Scorpions*, a book rich with possible connections to their lives, they were all strong enough readers to comprehend the text without difficulty, and they had all been supported in earlier discussions by me and their classroom teacher. Three of this group's members were especially conscientious students who had assumed leadership roles in previous discussion groups, they all had participated in successful literature discussion groups at some point during the school year, and they all had experienced numerous types of scaffolding and modeling by me, their teacher, and their classmates throughout the school year. Compounding my sense of dismay was the fact that I was a university professor who specialized in literature discussions. I had researched these discussions and used them extensively in my own teaching—I was the "expert." These types of discussions were not supposed to happen to me.

It is exactly these types of discussions, however, that intrigue me and keep me motivated to continue studying literature discussion groups in all their complexity. In this book, I hope to highlight the dilemmas and possibilities I encounter as I work to implement literature discussion groups both in my own classroom and in collaborative settings with other classroom teachers. The dilemmas that I address have arisen from listening to and observing my students as they engage in literature discussions, from asking them their perceptions and opinions, and from trying to make changes in literacy instruction within an institutional structure that does not always support such change. Rather than provide easy solutions to these problems, I hope to explore the many possible ways we can think about these issues; to provide opportunities for teachers to reflect on their own situations, students, and dilemmas; and to consider how the ideas discussed here might apply or be modified to apply to many teachers in many different teaching contexts. I hope to reveal the exciting possibilities that emerge for us and our students when we work to find ways of addressing these dilemmas and turning them into opportunities for learning and growth.

Reflection Point 1.1

Obtain a journal where you can reflect and record your ideas as you read through this book. In your journal, reflect on the following questions:

1. What would you like to see become possible in your literacy teaching?

2. What dilemmas are you currently facing in your efforts to make these possibilities a reality?

3. What would you like to see in your classroom regarding the use of literature discussion groups?

4. What questions or challenges are you facing in your use of literature discussion groups?

Keep your lists of possibilities, questions, and challenges in mind as you read through this book and compare them to the dilemmas I discuss. We will return to these lists at the end of the book to determine whether your questions have been addressed and your hoped-for possibilities seem more attainable.

Who Am I?

I began my teaching career as a third-grade teacher in a poor, rural school district in Nebraska, USA. I can still remember vividly the day I stood in front of my class teaching a skill from the mandated basal curriculum and thought to myself, "There has to be a better way to do this. If I'm bored by this, what must my students be feeling?" This was the impetus for my returning to graduate school to learn ways to be a more effective teacher. As a full-time graduate student, I reveled in all the new information about innovative teaching methods, and I found myself undergoing a profound shift in my beliefs about teaching and learning. Specifically, my doctoral studies at the University of Arizona influenced my beliefs about literacy instruction. I began to form a new philosophy that supported my belief that teaching from a basal might not be the most effective way to teach reading to students, especially those from diverse and non–English-speaking backgrounds.

As I learned about different types of reading instruction, I became intrigued by the instructional practice of literature discussion groups, and in particular, Eeds and Wells's (1989) notion of "grand conversations." Eeds and Wells argue that most children's experience with literature is similar to "gentle inquisitions" in which the discussion consists of the teacher asking questions and the students attempting to answer them, with comprehension judged by how closely students' answers match those in the textbook. In comparison to gentle inquistions, Eeds and Wells suggest that grand conversations occur when we allow for multiple interpretations of a text and encourage our students to construct and share their own meanings. This idea, that there can be several readings and interpretations of a text, is in "direct conflict with an inquisition model which assumes that a correct interpretation exists that is known to the teacher and is to be discovered by the students" (Eeds & Wells, 1989, p. 5). Eeds and Wells contend that when teachers allow students to share the meanings and interpretations they have created while reading a text, a deeper meaning and enriched understanding becomes possible for all students. Hence, the mere discussion becomes a "grand conversation."

As I read the examples of grand conversations from Eeds and Wells's research with fifth- and sixth-grade students, I thought to myself, "Yes! This is how I want my students to talk about literature." In these examples, I saw students working together to construct meanings and fill in the gaps in their comprehension. I heard students recount personal stories inspired by the reading or discussion that helped them develop a personal significance of the text. I saw students actively hypothesizing, interpreting, verifying, and questioning what they were reading in an effort to uncover meaning. For example, one group was actively working to determine the meaning of the word *dumbwaiter*, while another group was hypothesizing whether a character was an angel and using different text-based examples to support their hypothesis. While I read these discussion examples, however, a voice in my head kept reminding me that the discussions I heard my own former students having were a far cry from what I was reading. Consequently, I found Eeds and Wells's examples of grand conversations simultaneously inspiring and intimidating. I wondered what I needed to do differently to facilitate grand conversations among my own students. I knew such conversations did not just magically occur, yet I was unsure of how to start the process in my own classroom.

It was also during my doctoral studies that I became a research assistant for a study investigating upper elementary teachers' beliefs and practices regarding teaching reading comprehension (Richardson, Anders, Tidwell, & Lloyd, 1991). Through this research study I met Clay and Roxanne, two of the teachers who participated. These two fifth-grade teachers team taught and used literature discussion groups in their classroom. I was interested in how they used literature discussion groups as a way of structuring their literacy program, so at the conclusion of the study I asked if I could continue to work in their classroom to further explore some of my questions regarding these groups. I spent the following school year observing and working in their classroom as I completed my dissertation. Seeing literature discussion groups at work in Clay and Roxanne's classroom gave me concrete examples that helped my understanding of this instructional practice. However, this experience also gave me reason to question whether the glowing examples of student discussions found in research were complete reflections of what was actually happening in many classrooms. As I discussed my concerns with one of my professors, she remarked, "You're such a skeptic, Karen. But that's a good quality to have as a researcher." Looking back, I see that she was right. It was my skeptic voice that led me to conduct research in Clay and Roxanne's classroom. I wanted to see for myself if grand conversations were as easy to implement as the research implied, if students' discussions were always grand, and what types of conversations students had when the teacher was not present in their discussions.

As I continued my graduate studies, I became increasingly concerned about urban education issues. As someone who was planning a career as a teacher educator, I began to worry about how I would effectively prepare future teachers to teach in urban settings when I had never taught in such a setting myself. This concern propelled me to leave my graduate studies for a year and return to the classroom as a full-time fifth-grade teacher in a school in Tucson, Arizona, USA. During this year, I was able to experience firsthand the challenges of teaching in an urban setting and the complex task of trying to implement literature discussion groups.

After I graduated and began working as a university professor, I continued to explore the use of literature discussion groups by working collaboratively with classroom teachers who were attempting to implement this type of literacy instruction. In particular, I worked for a year with Marcy Hyllberg, a fifth-grade teacher in Racine, Wisconsin, USA as she worked to make changes to her literacy program. My experiences as a doctoral student and classroom teacher in Tucson allowed me to more effectively support Marcy in her efforts to use literature discussion groups.

Why Am I Writing This Book?

When I first encountered examples of literature discussion groups and grand conversations in my doctoral research, I was both inspired and overwhelmed. Although I wanted to believe in the power of this instructional practice, I had a difficult time reconciling the research examples with examples from my own teaching. The research made the students' discussions sound almost profound and gave the impression that getting students to have this type of discussion was an effortless task. However, my own experiences as a teacher caused me to raise some questions. Were literature discussion groups always this fabulous, this in-depth, this thought-provoking? As a teacher, I knew things did not always go perfectly in my classroom, regardless of how wonderful the instructional practice. Where were the examples of discussion groups that did not go so well? Where were the articles that would address the struggles and difficulties teachers encountered? Were literature discussions always this easy to implement? If so, did the fact that my students did not have these types of grand conversations make me a bad teacher?

Questions like these have propelled me to continue studying literature discussion groups over the last 10 years, and they are the motivation behind my writing this book. I want teachers to see not only the amazing possibilities that exist when using literature discussion groups, but also the messy, difficult dilemmas that arise when trying to implement discussion groups into literacy instruction. As I discovered, achieving the types of conversations found in the research is anything but easy. Students' conversations are not always grand; the discussions are not always in-depth and multifaceted. However, these not-so-optimal discussions provided me with an opportunity to reflect on how I was using discussion groups, to evaluate how discussion groups were influencing my students' literacy learning, and, most of all, to hear what my students were trying to tell me when their discussions did not meet my grand expectations. Through listening to my students, I have learned a tremendous amount about what it takes to implement literature discussion groups and the possibilities that exist for students when they are allowed to engage in this type of literacy context. I hope that by balancing the possibilities with the dilemmas, this book will provide a realistic portrait for teachers who are attempting to implement literature discussion groups into their literacy instruction. It is not an easy or simple task, but I have found that the rewards far outweigh the difficulties encountered along the way.

My Beliefs About Reading Instruction and Literacy Learning

My experiences as a teacher and researcher have helped me to better understand the possibilities and dilemmas that exist when using literature discussion groups. They also have helped clarify my beliefs regarding literacy instruction for the upper elementary grades and the role of literature discussion in that instruction. My own personal experience with reading, however, also has influenced my beliefs. Even as a young child I was an avid reader. I was the child who always had her nose in a book and was frequently found late at night reading in bed with a flashlight. Although my family did not have much money for "extras," my mother always scraped together enough spare change for me to order one book each month from the school book orders. I grew up valuing books for the places they could take me, the characters I could meet, and the adventures I could experience vicariously through reading. I knew what it felt like to read a book that was simply too good to put down, to finish a book that was so good you felt you would burst if you could not talk about it. I wanted my students to feel the same way about reading. As a young teacher, however, I was disheartened by the number of students who did not share my love of reading and had never felt moved enough by a book to not want to put it down. After several months of reading the selections in the district's basals, I could better understand why my students had never experienced the power and joy of reading if such texts were their primary exposure to reading. As a result, I felt even more compelled to seek out meaningful ways of engaging my students in the reading process. These experiences as a reader, teacher, and researcher have all melded together to create in me a set of beliefs regarding the teaching and learning of literacy. I will discuss my beliefs more thoroughly in the next section, but I would first invite you to reflect in your journal about your own beliefs as a teacher of reading.

Reflection Point 1.2_____

Take a moment to think about the following questions:

1. What are your beliefs regarding how to most effectively teach reading?

2. What are your beliefs about how students best learn to read?

3. What are your experiences as a reader? How might these experiences be influencing your beliefs and how you teach reading in your classroom?

4. What goals do you have for your students as readers and how do you see literature discussion groups as a way of meeting these goals?

When you read the book, you're reading it with yourself. If there's a word you don't know, you have to try it by yourself. If you're reading like with a partner, you don't know what the word's about, you could ask your partner, and then you could learn it.

Maria

Because this way when we understand other people's points, we have an expansion on what we think of books and then we start to read them more and then to start asking other people if they've read the book and what they thought about it.

Jamie

Sometimes you know we don't like things. Like, if you gave me a book that I didn't like and I *had* to read it, I would, like, have a long face.

Alana

These quotes were taken from interviews with my fifth-grade class in Tucson regarding their thoughts on how we were "doing literacy" in our classroom. As I listened to the students, I was amazed at how closely their comments reflected my own personal beliefs about literacy teaching and learning. As you read this section, I encourage you to think about how the above comments illustrate these beliefs.

Above all, I believe that reading is a constructive process that is influenced by the prior knowledge, life experiences, interests, and perspectives a reader brings to any given text. Readers do not simply "take" information from a text; rather, their experiences and attitudes interact with the text to create a meaning that is unique to that individual. Louise Rosenblatt (1978), whose work has greatly influenced my thinking, called this process a *transaction*—both bringing meaning to and taking meaning from a text. Because each reader's experiences and knowledge are different, any text is always open to multiple interpretations. By emphasizing the multiple interpretations of a text, we can help our students understand the constructive, active nature of reading.

I also believe that learning is a social process that is influenced by the context and cultural factors present in any context. This is exemplified by Vygotsky's (1934/1978) notion of the zone of proximal development (ZPD) in his sociocultural theory. Vygotsky defines the ZPD as the distance between a child's independent developmental level and the child's level of potential development when supported by collaboration with a more capable peer. The teacher often assumes the role of more capable peer, but as Maria's comment illustrates, fellow classmates can also serve in this role. The notion of learning as a social process also fits well with a constructivist notion of reading. As students share their interpretations of text, their individual understanding can take new forms and facilitate their thinking, or as Jamie put it, result in "an expansion on what we think of the book."

Although as teachers we often focus on how students' intellectual interactions contribute to their learning, I believe it is important to remember that cultural and social factors, such as gender, ethnicity, and power relations, also influence the learning that occurs in any context. For example, does it matter to students whether their learning partners are boys or girls? How does a student's ethnicity and cultural experiences influence the meanings that are derived from a text? Are some students' interpretations given more credibility than others? Whose voices are heard the loudest and given the most attention when sharing interpretations? These types of social and cultural issues will be developed further in Chapter 6.

Because I am committed to enacting democratic principles in my classroom (Apple & Bean, 1995; Dewey, 1938), I believe it is important to give students a voice in determining the course of their literacy learning. One way of doing this is to allow students to choose the books they will read for literacy instruction. As Alana's comment suggests, this is an important aspect for many students and facilitates their ability to find personal relevance and meaning in the books they read. The notion of relevance is important to me as a teacher: When students read a book that is relevant to their own lives, it increases the likelihood that they will be able to draw from their personal experiences in interpreting the text. Being able to find this type of personal meaning in books has greatly enhanced many of my students' motivation for reading and has helped them experience the personal pleasure and discovery that can be found in books.

These beliefs will be woven throughout the remainder of the book. I think it is important to emphasize that these beliefs have been influenced by the experiences I have had with my students—listening to what they say about our literacy instruction, watching how they respond to books they choose to read, and listening to how they talk about such books. In other words, my beliefs have been influenced and strengthened by keeping my students in sight as I teach literacy in my classroom.

Reflection Point 1.3

For the next several days during your literacy instruction time, make a special effort to listen to what your students say during this time, how they act, and what their emotions are. What are students telling you about how they experience your instruction? Is what students say consistent with your beliefs about literacy teaching and learning?

People and Places Represented in This Book

Throughout this book you will hear students' voices from the three fifth-grade classrooms in which I explored literature discussion groups: Clay and Roxanne's (team teachers), my own, and Marcy's. In this section I briefly describe the classrooms to provide a sense of the larger cultural and economic context of each school, and I highlight a few students from each classroom whose voices you will hear frequently throughout the book.

Classroom 1. This classroom was located in a multiethnic school in Tucson, Arizona with a large population of Hispanic or Latino/a students. There was a considerable number of Native American students in the school as well. Roxanne and Clay had combined their classes by opening the wall partition that separated their individual classrooms, and they team taught for the majority of the school day. I observed their classroom two or three times per week for the first semester of the school year, and I began collecting more formal data in the second semester. During this semester, I was in the classroom every day during literature time. I sat with discussion groups, conducted informal interviews with students, and videotaped a discussion group each day. Mimi and Jonathan are two students from this classroom who you will read about.

Mimi was a petite girl with nonstop energy. In contrast to many of her Hispanic female classmates, she was assertive and enjoyed being the center of attention. Mimi was not a particularly strong reader, and she preferred hands-on activities and playing sports during recess.

Jonathan was a tall, lanky Caucasian boy with an easy-going manner and a tendency toward sarcasm. Jonathan's passion was cars and anything related to mechanics. He frequently had difficulty comprehending his literature books, but he would discuss articles from his auto mechanics and sports car magazines at length.

Classroom 2. The second classroom that informed this book was my own fifth-grade classroom in Tucson, Arizona. This classroom was also in a multiethnic, urban school where the majority of students received free or reduced-price lunches. Our class consisted of students from many different ethnic backgrounds, including Caucasian, Hispanic, African American, Native American, Asian, and Middle Eastern. The community in which my students lived was plagued with the problems found in many urban neighborhoods: poverty, violence, homelessness, gangs, and drugs. I used literature discussion groups throughout the year with my students and was constantly collecting observation notes on their discussions and reflecting in a teacher journal. A specific focus of my reflection was on how we were using peer and self-assessments in our literature study. At the end of each book, students completed both a self-evaluation and a peer evaluation on the members of their discussion group. My decision to include this type of assessment was influenced by my belief that students need opportunities to engage in self-evaluation as a way to help them take ownership of their learning and facilitate their efforts to become self-regulated learners. To gain students' perspectives regarding how they were experiencing both the literature discussion groups and our method of assessment, I interviewed each of my students individually in January and again in May. The students from my classroom whose voices you will hear frequently are Deonte, Maria, and Matt.

Deonte was a transfer student who came to our school with a long history of problems, both academic and behavioral, and a brilliant smile. He was obsessed with basketball, had tremendous athletic ability, and was convinced he was going to make it to the NBA. A biracial child, Deonte lived in a crime-ridden housing project with his Caucasian mother, and he had never known his African American father. Deonte struggled with identity issues and his search for an identity and culture was evident in many of his behavioral problems. Deonte also had difficulty dealing with his anger. The first few weeks of school he would frequently sit at his desk and break pencils in half or bang his head against the wall because he was so filled with anger and he did not know how to cope with it. It was no surprise that his academic record was filled with negative assessments. Helping Deonte learn to deal with his anger and begin to develop an identity that he could be proud of was one of the most rewarding experiences of my teaching career.

Maria was a quiet ESL student whose family had immigrated to the United States from Mexico. Maria's parents did not speak English but were still very involved in her education and attended all the school activities. Maria struggled with comprehension but always maintained a positive attitude and frequently partner-read with other students to help with the reading demands of our literacy program. Her academic difficulties, language barriers, and overweight frame caused Maria to have low self-esteem. She loved receiving any type of positive attention, and I could always count on getting a hug from her as she came into my room in the morning and left at the end of the day.

Matt and his mother had recently moved to Tucson from California. With his sun-bleached blonde hair, deep blue eyes, and devilish, slightly crooked smile, Matt looked the part of a soap opera star and had an attitude to match. Although many teachers found his somewhat smart-mouthed attitude annoying, Matt and I hit it off immediately. I delighted in his quick wit and dry sense of humor, discovering a young boy with a tremendous need to be loved behind his sarcastic exterior. Matt and his mother lived in near destitute conditions in a one-room shack that contained no furniture but a worn-out sofa and a mattress pad on the floor. Matt worked selling newspapers on the street corner and I often saw him at his post early in the morning as I came to work, in the evening as I drove home, and often on weekends as well.

Classroom 3. In this classroom I worked collaboratively with Marcy, the classroom teacher, to help her find ways of integrating literature-based instruction with the more skills-focused instruction she was currently using. Marcy had been a graduate student of mine while working on her master's degree, and after graduation we agreed to work together in her classroom to address the questions she had about how best to use literature discussion groups with her students. Marcy's students were predominately Caucasian, with approximately 25% of the students either African American or Hispanic. The school was located in a predominately working class neighborhood in Racine, Wisconsin and the majority of the students came from working-class or poverty-level homes. I was a member of Marcy's classroom two or three mornings each week for the entire school year. I took observation notes, sat in with discussion groups, cotaught lessons, videotaped discussion groups, and met with the groups to reflect as they watched videotaped segments of their discussions from the previous day. Through the students' reflections we were able to see how they were experiencing their discussion groups; what they liked, what they wanted to change, what was helpful, and what was hindering their ability to have productive discussions. The students from Marcy's classroom who you will hear from throughout this book are Noelia, Hannah, Michael, and Jessie.

Noelia was a delightful student. Intelligent with an open, trusting nature, she could always be counted on to "tell it like it was." She enjoyed reading and was always an active participant in literature discussions. Noelia usually could be found with several *Teen* or *Tiger Beat* magazines in her desk, which she loved to discuss with her friends—along with the newest shade of nail polish—during any break in the day.

Hannah was a shy, sensitive, overweight girl who often looked as if she was carrying the weight of the world on her shoulders. Hannah and her mother, and often one of her mother's boyfriends, lived in an apartment above a local pizza parlor. Hannah was frequently left alone in the evenings when her mother and boyfriend went out to the bars. Her mother often was not home before Hannah left for school and Hannah worried tremendously about her mother's safety when this happened.

Michael joined Marcy's classroom in November when his mother remarried and moved to Racine. Michael was a bright, articulate boy who excelled in school and was viewed as a leader by his peers. A gifted reader, he was an active participant in his literature discussion groups in which he often assumed a leadership position.

Jessie was an outspoken, vibrant girl who loved to talk and give her opinion on any topic. She usually was an eager participant in her literature discussion groups; however, she occasionally allowed allegiance to her friends to interfere with the task at hand. One of her good friends often defiantly refused to read or participate in her group and Jessie, caught in the bind of wanting to participate but also to be faithful to her friend, often chose to side with her friend and did not read the book or discuss it with her group.

These are the classrooms and students that have influenced my thinking about literature discussion groups. As you read subsequent chapters of this book, you will hear their voices as they share their perceptions and thoughts regarding their experiences as discussion group participants. I hope that you will find their voices as enlightening as I have.

Organization of the Rest of This Book

Using literature discussion groups in your classroom can be simultaneously exciting and frustrating. Many of you are already experimenting with discussion groups and have an idea of the particular possibilities and dilemmas that surround this instructional practice. I hope the ideas discussed here will further your thinking as you start, or continue, to use literature discussion groups with your students. In the remaining chapters I will present the following topics:

Chapter 2: There is a growing theoretical and empirical base that supports the use of literature discussions as a component of our literacy instruction. This chapter presents the theoretical framework that guides this book and the instructional practice of literature discussions. I also will describe several different models that have been developed for structuring literature discussions in our classrooms, and I describe in detail the instructional model that was used in both my classroom and Marcy's.

Chapter 3: In this chapter I discuss and illustrate how I used different types of scaffolding, modeling, and demonstrations to help move my students beyond the traditional round-robin type of discussions. Included will be the issue of how some types of scaffolding have the potential to become crutches that result in the types of discussions they are trying to eliminate.

Chapter 4: A common dilemma that many teachers encounter is that of how to cover the mandated curriculum skills while using literature-based practices in their literacy instruction. This chapter presents examples of how skills such as story structure, vocabulary, theme, and character perspectives might be taught within a framework of a literature discussion group.

Chapter 5: Although much has been written about different ways to assess students' literacy abilities, far less has been written about the assessment of students' individual abilities and development within the context of literature discussion groups, as well as the effectiveness of the overall groups themselves. This chapter describes assessment practices that are consistent with the theory and philosophy underlying the instructional practice of literature discussions, and provides examples of both teacher assessments and student self- and peer assessments. How such assessments might be used to inform more standard forms of assessment, such as report cards, also is discussed.

Chapter 6: Attending to the cognitive aspects of literature discussions is a necessary, but not sufficient, part of planning for and implementing literature discussion groups. Because literature discussions are an inherently social context, social and cultural factors are present and have the potential to influence how students experience their learning opportunities in such contexts. This chapter addresses how such social and cultural factors impact students' perceptions of literature discussions and the learning environments that exist in discussion groups.

Although the chapters are organized in a particular order, this does not mean the book needs to be read in a sequential manner. Depending on your experience with literature discussion groups, you may choose to begin with whichever chapter addresses a specific dilemma or possibility that you have encountered in your own teaching. I also want to stress that this book is not intended to serve as a "recipe" for implementing literature discussion groups, nor do I present *the* correct way of using them. Rather, I draw from the research and my own experience to present several possibilities and dilemmas that exist when using literature discussion groups and, hopefully, I provide a chance for you to think about your own practice and its impact on your students in new and exciting ways.

Why Should I Use Literature Discussion Groups, and How Do I Implement Them in My Classroom?

> *I observed the Sharing Susan group today. They were animatedly discussing the whole issue of finding out that the parents who had raised you were not really your parents. At one point in the discussion, Noelia burst out and said with great emotion, "All I know is that if someone told me my parents, who I've lived with my whole life and raised me and loved me, gave me a home and clothing—(her voice is breaking here and tears welling in her eyes)—if anyone told me they were not my parents, I could never leave them and go with someone else." This seemed to be the general sentiment of the group. Students considered their parents to be their parents because they raised them and loved them. They thought Susan should be able to stay with her "real" parents and not be forced to go with her birth parents. It was a fabulously rich and meaningful discussion.*

The event described in this vignette occurred the first time Marcy and I attempted to use literature discussion groups in her classroom. Listening to Noelia's heartfelt statement reminded me again of the power of allowing students to discuss personally meaningful books. In my work with literature groups, I have had such experiences many times—hearing students connect with texts and talk about them in ways that further their thinking about the issues and ideas found in those books. Rosenblatt (1978) calls this type of reading *aesthetic reading*—an experience during which the reader pays attention to the images, feelings, and attitudes aroused by the text.

It is possible to take an aesthetic stance toward reading without actually discussing the text. My experience, however, has led me to believe that students benefit greatly from being able to talk about their responses to books and hear other people's responses. While listening to their discussions, I frequently hear students talk about difficult issues and personal experiences that never find their way into their literature logs or written responses. Rather, these responses seem to be prompted by the act of discussing the book with their peers. Discussions appear to be generative, synergistic environments where students are able to talk about their responses to books in ways that are not revealed in other formats.

The following notes from my observation journal focus on Hannah and her group and reveal another example of aesthetic reading. The students are reading a story titled *Monkey Island* (Fox, 1991) about a young boy's efforts to find the mother who has left him alone in a large city.

> Today the group kept asking why Clay didn't just call the police for help. Hannah responded by saying that he might not because if his mom did come back and the police knew she had been gone, they might take him away from her and he didn't want his mom to get into trouble by calling the police. I can't help but think that her interpretation and inference is coming from her own situation with her mother and being left alone so much but not wanting to tell anyone because she doesn't want to get her mom into trouble. She also knows the legal consequences of a child being taken away from the parents if the police find out they have abandoned a child, even temporarily. This was definitely an eye-opener for her group and a perspective none of them had even considered.

This example reveals how, for Hannah, reading this book is a lived-through experience—the emotions and interpretations triggered by the events in the book are directly relevant to her own personal experiences. Furthermore, the discussion group is a place for her to express this lived-through experience and use her personal experiences as a way for members of her group to better understand what happens in the book. The springboard nature of discussion groups, where one person's question creates an opportunity for other people to share their interpretations and experiences, is at the heart of what occurs in literature discussion groups and is the reason why they are so much more powerful than having students read and respond to literature individually. The multiple interpretations that exist when reading any text create opportunities for students to understand books in exciting new ways. As a result, when students share their varied interpretations they are socially constructing the meaning of what they have read. If students only read and respond individually, these opportunities for sharing multiple perspectives and constructing new interpretations are lost.

Reflection Point 2.1 _____

For the next several days, pay special attention to the ways in which your students respond to what they read. Do you hear evidence of aesthetic reading? Are students using their personal experiences to inform their interpretations of their books? Are students allowed to use discussion as a way to reveal and discuss multiple perspectives of what they are reading?

Students' Perspectives

> Having a discussion beats paper! 'Cause papers don't talk back!
> Ryan

When I asked my class of fifth-graders in Tuscon to share their thoughts about how we were using literature discussion groups, they were more than willing to give me an earful. Fortunately, they overwhelmingly enjoyed engaging in discussion groups and their responses provided me with further support for using this type of literacy instruction. In this section, I describe their responses as they relate to two main themes: (1) literature discussions were more enjoyable than doing worksheets, and (2) engaging in literature discussions helped them become better readers.

"Old Way" = Boring, Discussions = Fun

> I like this because you don't have to sit at your desk and be bored and read it by yourself. I think we did it this way to have fun reading books.
>
> Deonte

> This way we can make it a little bit funner instead of just passing out the sheets and just answering the questions like the boring old way.
>
> Matt

> I think why we did it this way was to get us started in a new way instead of doing the old way...we could have our chance to pick our own books and get into the books that were on our level that we thought was interesting and not just answering the old boring stuff.
>
> Maria

As the students' responses reveal, many felt that having literature discussion groups was more fun than what they called the "old" way of doing reading. For most students, the old way meant reading a book individually, or everyone in the class round-robin reading the same book and doing worksheets or answering questions in writing about the book. Students were adamant in their dislike for the old method, which often was described as "boring." What was interesting to me was that many of my students' previous experiences with the "old way" were not with traditional basal textbooks, as you might suspect, but rather with literature books that had been "basalized" by the way their teachers were using them. My students talked about reading their literature book and then having to do "packets." I discovered that the packets their teachers had constructed to go along with the books were very similar to traditional basal worksheets. They contained exercises that included vocabulary words that students had to define and use in sentences, and comprehension-check questions that had to be answered in complete sentences. The students completed these packets individually and that is what constituted "reading."

As a teacher, I understand the appeal of such packets because they represent one way of addressing the skills we are compelled to teach in our literacy programs. However, my students' negative views toward the packets made me question whether they really learned many of the skills the packets taught. I know many of you are probably thinking, "But I have to teach my students skills." I had the same dilemma and I describe an alternative for how we might teach skills within a literature-based system more fully in Chapter 4.

As I listened to my students talk with such disdain about this type of system, I realized that simply using quality literature with them was not enough—it all hinged on *how* the literature was being used. My students were clear in their preference for being able to talk about their books rather than just doing worksheets. Having students meet in discussion groups helped me put my beliefs about reading into action, because my students were much more likely to construct their own personal meaning, share multiple interpretations, and use each other as resources for learning when they were in groups—rather than alone at their desks filling out worksheets.

Discussions = Better Readers

Although I was glad to hear that my students enjoyed engaging in literature discussions, simply having fun was not enough. As a teacher, I also needed to know that my students were growing as readers from this instructional method. Thankfully, my students also revealed their belief that they were becoming better readers due to the opportunity to discuss books with their groups.

> I think it helps me because sometimes when I read I get lost and I just keep on reading and then after I stop [and discuss], it helps me to remember what happened.
>
> Risa

> I think we get better at reading, we can get to a higher reading level and it helps us with our vocabulary and our writing. You get to hear other people's ideas and some facts you didn't know, like if it has something in common with another person, they can share that.
>
> Matt

> It helped me comprehend the books a little better and understand other points of view and have more ways to look at the book than my own.
>
> Jamie

> I like it better than just silent reading because you can discuss it with somebody else and all these people are reading the same books and it's [helpful to be able to talk with them] because you know more things 'cuz they notice things you would never notice and you just learn your mistakes and how to read better and words you didn't know and it makes you a better reader.
>
> Jackie

These students' comments helped me know that my students were growing as readers through engaging in literature discussions. Hearing multiple perspectives broadened students' understanding of what they were reading and being able to discuss the books helped them clarify their understanding and remember what they had read. Risa's comment was especially important to me because she was an ESL student who struggled with reading. Listening to her talk about how discussing the books helped her to comprehend what she was reading allayed my worries about how literature discussion groups were supporting her growth.

My observations in all three classrooms in which I worked support the students' perspectives. I watched and listened to students actively and animatedly talk about what they were reading, rely on each other for help in clarifying understanding, and explore alternative interpretations with their group members as a way to extend their thinking about the book. These observations helped solidify my beliefs about reading and showed me how such beliefs work in real classrooms. In the next section I describe several models for how teachers could organize their literature discussion groups, as well as the framework that I used in my classroom.

Literature Discussion Groups—What Are They?

There are numerous models for how you might organize literature discussion groups in your classroom. In this section I briefly describe three of the models that have influenced my thinking and instructional practices. In Box 2.1 you will find several resources that describe these and other models in more detail. I encourage you to explore the different models found in these sources and decide which ideas fit with your own personal beliefs about literacy teaching and learning.

Book Club

Book Club (Raphael, Pardo, Highfield, & McMahon, 1997) incorporates two theoretical foundations that are consistent with the theories underlying this book: social constructivism and reader response. The creators of Book Club believe that learning is a social process and that students use their prior knowledge and experiences to interact with text and construct

Box 2.1
Resources for Organizing Literature Discussion Groups

Daniels, H. (1994). *Literature circles: Voice and choice in the student-centered classroom.* York, ME: Stenhouse.

Dugan, J. (1997). Transactional literature discussions: Engaging students in the appreciation and understanding of literature. *The Reading Teacher, 51,* 4–29.

Gambrell, L.B., & Almasi, J.F. (1996). *Lively discussions! Fostering engaged reading.* Newark, DE: International Reading Association.

O'Flahavan, J. (1994/1995). Teacher role options in peer discussions about literature. *The Reading Teacher, 48,* 354–356.

Raphael, T.E., & McMahon, S.I. (1994). Book Club: An alternative framework for reading instruction. *The Reading Teacher, 48,* 102–116.

Raphael, T.E., Pardo, L.S., Highfield, K., & McMahon, S.I. (1997). *Book Club: A literature-based curriculum.* Littleton, MA: Small Planet Communications.

Roser, N.L., & Martinez, M.G. (1995). *Book talk and beyond: Children and teachers respond to literature.* Newark, DE: International Reading Association.

Short, K.G., & Pierce, K. (1990). *Talking about books: Creating literate communities.* Portsmouth, NH: Heinemann.

Wiencek, J., & O'Flahavan, J. (1994). From teacher-led to peer discussions about literature: Suggestions for making the shift. *Language Arts, 71(7),* 488–498.

personally meaningful understandings of and responses to what they read. There are four components of Book Club: reading, writing, community share (whole-class discussion), and book clubs (small group discussions). Instruction is woven into all four components. The creators of Book Club emphasize that while these four components are the framework for the model, how teachers actually choose to sequence and implement them is up to the individual teacher's discretion.

The reading component involves selecting a wide variety of excellent literature that provides opportunities for many types of reading (i.e., independent, with peers, in small groups), along with choosing a teacher read-aloud book. The writing component encourages students to respond to their reading in open-ended ways. The Book Club emphasizes three categories of literature response: personal (reader's emotional response, personal experiences); creative (imaginative ideas a reader explores as a result of reading); and critical (analyzing the author's use of literary techniques). Book Club encourages these types of written responses through reading logs and think sheets. Reading logs are a place for students to record their responses to what they are reading, and the main purpose of the logs is to focus students' attention on ideas that can support a lively discussion. A think sheet is an open-ended worksheet that introduces students to new ways of thinking about the text and new ways of organizing their thoughts. For example, a think sheet might ask students to predict outcomes, identify a theme, analyze a character, create a plot-action graph, or make connections between texts.

Community share is a whole-class discussion in which teachers and students can bring ideas from their reading, writing, and small-group discussions to the entire class. This is an opportunity for teachers to introduce new ideas to students, address misconceptions students have formed based on their reading, share thoughts and feelings, and also enhance the sense of community in the classroom. Community share can be done either before or after the book club discussions depending on the teacher's instructional purpose.

Book clubs are the small-group discussions at the heart of the Book Club framework. The other components all serve to support the students' efforts to engage in real and meaningful conversations about what they have read. Raphael, Pardo, Highfield, and McMahon (1997) emphasize the importance of providing instruction for students to help them develop the conversational skills necessary for a successful book club discussion. Information about how to incorporate this type of instruction, as well as instruction directly related to reading and writing skills, is described in more detail in Raphael et al.'s *Book Club: A Literature-Based Curriculum* (see Box 2.1).

Conversational Discussion Groups

The Conversational Discussion Group (CDG) (Wiencek & O'Flahavan, 1994) was developed in part to help teachers relinquish their social and interpretive authority in literature discussions with their students. The CDG approach facilitates students' ability to develop both social interaction norms (i.e., do not interrupt), and literary interpretations (i.e., character motive, theme). The CDG framework utilizes groups of students ranging in size from four to six members, and includes three phases: opening, discussion, and debriefing. The day before a discussion, students read a piece of literature and write a response in a literature response log. The next day, the group meets to discuss the reading. In the opening phase, the teacher leads the students in a discussion of social norms (e.g., How can we get along as a group?) and interpretative orientations (e.g., What can we talk about?). Student responses are recorded on a chart under the headings *interaction* (for social norms) and *interpretation* (for interpretative orientations). Each time the group meets, the chart is reviewed and new ideas for social norms and interpretations are added.

The teacher then leaves the group and students begin the discussion phase, using their texts and written responses as resources for their discussion. As students talk, the teacher sits outside the group and records how the group manages its discussion. After a specified time period (e.g., 15 minutes), the teacher rejoins the group and leads students in a debriefing during which they share specifics about both the social norms and interpretations in their discussion. During this phase the teacher also helps students develop an understanding of literary language by introducing terms such as *character motive* when students discuss the intent behind a character's action. As students become more adept at using CDG, the teacher engages in the process less frequently, and the two-column chart becomes less of a focus.

Transactional Literature Discussions

In Transactional Literature Discussions (TLD), the goal is for "students and teachers to understand the story by transacting with the text and interacting with each other" (Dugan, 1997, p. 87). TLDs are cycles of literacy events that include the elements of Getting Ready, Reading and Thinking Aloud, Wondering on Paper, Talking, Thinking on Paper, and Looking Back. Getting Ready involves prereading activities such as selecting books, activating background knowledge, creating interest in the texts, and making predictions. In Reading and Thinking Aloud, the teacher models thinking aloud while reading in order to illuminate for students the thought processes used to make sense of a text. Rather than stopping at predetermined points in the story to ask questions, teachers encourage students to think aloud whenever they have a question or response while reading.

Wondering on Paper is a short written response to the story that is created either during or immediately after the reading. These wonderings allow students to revisit their initial responses at a later time, and they set the agenda for the talk sessions that come next. In the Talking sessions, students and teachers share their wonderings, respond to each other's ideas, and jointly construct meanings of the text. To facilitate discussion, students use the RQL2 strategy (Respond, Question, Listen, and Link). Each part of RQL2 has ideas for how students might participate. For example, the following items are listed under Respond: Say what you liked or disliked, Tell about your favorite part, and Tell how the story made you feel (see Dugan, 1997, for a description of Question, Listen, and Link components). RQL2 is posted on a chart so that students and the teacher can refer to it during talk sessions.

After the talk session, students select one idea/topic/theme to further explore in their journals—what is referred to as Thinking on Paper. Dugan advises that to make the writing as meaningful as possible, students should have opportunities to share their journals with peers and the teacher, and to receive feedback on their ideas. The last element of the TLD approach is Looking Back, in which teachers encourage students to evaluate their learning by reflecting on the reading and writing events that occurred that day. This might involve verbal reflection on what they learned, summarizing the story that was read, confirming/disconfirming their predictions, or suggesting ways to make the activities more meaningful.

Reflection Point 2.2

Compare the three frameworks discussed in this section to the system you are currently using, or thinking about using, in your own classroom. Look for similarities and differences and jot down questions that you have regarding how you might implement literature discussion groups in your classroom.

My Classroom

The framework I used in my classroom is not a pure example of any one of these models, but rather a compilation of features from many different models that I modified and adapted to fit my students' needs and my own teaching style and beliefs. Because many of my students were unfamiliar with literature discussion groups, I began the school year by using our class read-aloud novel as a way to begin demonstrating the skills they would need. At particular points in the book, I stopped and asked a discussion question or provided a prompt. Students could then discuss the question with the people in their seating group (students' desks were arranged in groups). We would then come back together as a class and discuss the various groups' interpretations of the question. For example, when we were reading the book *Tuck Everlasting* (Babbitt, 1975), a story about a family that has found a potion that allows whoever drinks it to live forever and never get older, I asked my students if they would drink the potion if given the opportunity. Students discussed their responses and reasons in their groups and then we came back together as a whole class to see what reasons students offered for wanting to drink, or not drink, the potion.

This process allowed students a chance to get comfortable with having a structured minidiscussion. Deciding when to shift from structured read-aloud book discussions to literature discussion groups is a personal decision that each teacher should make based on the knowledge she has about her students. My own preference would be to shift sooner rather than later, because I do not see these types of discussion skills as prerequisites students need prior to engaging in their own literature discussion groups. Rather, I see them as emerging skills that will continue to develop throughout the school year. As Galda, Rayburn, and Stanzi (2000) state in *Looking Through the Faraway End: Creating a Literature-Based Reading Curriculum With Second Graders*, you just have to "jump right in!" (p. 18). I hope the description that follows will give you ideas for how you might plan your big jump.

Before I begin, there are a couple of points to keep in mind as you read my description. Although many of the models present literature discussion groups that are facilitated by the teacher (i.e., the teacher is present during the discussion to support students' conversations), the discussion groups I used with my fifth graders (and Marcy's fifth graders) were peer-led. I had several different discussion groups going at the same time—consequently, I circulated through the room and sat in with various groups, but I was not with one specific group for the duration of their discussion. I also want to emphasize that implementing literature discussion groups is not a static process. The framework I used in my first attempt in my classrooom in Tuscon is not the same as the framework that Marcy and I eventually developed. The basic elements of the framework were the same, but we continued to refine and modify it based on the individual students in the classroom that year and our growing understanding of how to use this type of instructional practice. Do not be afraid that you will not "get it right" the first time. There is no right or wrong way to implement literature discussions. The main thing is that you take a leap of faith, knowing that you can make changes as you go.

It All Starts With the Books

> Marcy was going to wait until after Thanksgiving to start the next cycle, but I talked to Scott, Pete, and Jessie and they all wanted to start right away. They asked me when they were going to choose their next book and were disappointed when I told them not until after Thanksgiving. I told Marcy about the students' reactions and she asked the class what they wanted to do. The overwhelming majority wanted to start right away. I overheard numerous students talking about what book they wanted to read. I heard Jessie say, "I hope I get to read *Sharing Susan* next time. I'm dying to read that book!" It's great to hear their enthusiasm for various books and their eagerness to start a new book.

Organizing literature discussion groups begins with selecting the books. As the preceding excerpt from my journal illustrates, getting students to engage in powerful discussions of literature often hinges on finding books that will "hook" students in and motivate them to read. At the beginning of each discussion cycle, I selected 7 to 10 books from which students would choose the book they wanted to read. I tried to select a variety of topics and difficulty levels. If there were titles that students were already familiar with from previous grades, they had several other titles to choose from. Some students may have been exposed to the books in past years, but were not able to read them independently at the lower grade levels. By offering those texts again, students were provided with the opportunity to read them independently and create a new understanding of the book based on their own, and their group members', interpretations. To help address this potential concern, I encourage you to talk with your colleagues in the lower grades and see what titles they are using in their literacy instruction.

In building my literature collection, I relied on former students' recommendations for books they liked, as well as other teachers' recommendations. Another good source is the International Reading Association's *Children's Choices*, a compilation of books recommended by actual students that is published annually in the October issue of *The Reading Teacher*. I found I was able to build a good-sized library in a short period of time through ordering from publisher book clubs and using my bonus points to buy multiple copies of good titles. Many teachers buy hardbound copies of books due to the wear and tear they will receive, but I needed to build a library from scratch in a short period of time, so I opted for paperback copies because they were less expensive. These paperback books do show evidence of wear; however, they are still being used after 4 years. I found that the students were so excited about having their own individual copies of "real" books that they were more likely to be conscientious in how they took care of them. Box 2.2 contains examples of the types of texts that were offered as possibilities during one cycle of literature discussions in my fifth-grade classroom in Tuscon.

Box 2.2
Books for Use in Literature Discussion Groups

Blume, J. (1980). *Superfudge*. New York: Dell.
Bunting, E. (1991). *Sharing Susan*. New York: HarperCollins.
Byars, B.C. (1985). *Cracker Jackson*. New York: Viking.
Cleary, B. (1991). *Strider*. Ill. P.O. Zelinsky. New York: William Morrow.
Cooney, C. (1991). *Face on the milk carton*. New York: Laurel Leaf.
Naylor, P.R. (1991). *Shiloh*. New York: Bantam Doubleday Dell.
Paterson, K. (1978). *The great Gilly Hopkins*. New York: The Trumpet Club.
Rockwell, T. (1973). *How to eat fried worms*. New York: Bantam Doubleday Dell.
Rockwell, T. (1991). *How to get fabulously rich*. New York: Yearling.
Smith, R.K. (1972). *Chocolate fever*. New York: Bantam Doubleday Dell.

It is important to point out that the discussion groups explored in this book, from both my and Marcy's classrooms, were primarily reading realistic fiction. I did incorporate nonfiction texts into our literature discussion groups in my Tucson class, however, these discussion groups will not be addressed in this book. Although they are not specifically mentioned here, I would certainly encourage you to consider using different genres in your classroom. Using different genres can help generate powerful discussions and also promote integration of ideas across content areas. For an example of nonfiction and realistic fiction texts that I used in my classroom in Tuscon in conjunction with a social studies unit on the U.S. Civil War or World War II, refer to the sources in Box 2.3.

Box 2.3
Nonfiction and Historical Fiction Texts for Literature Discussions That Relate to the Civil War
(these are a combination of historical fiction and nonfiction picture books)

Adler, D. (1992). *A picture book of Harriet Tubman*. New York: Scholastic.
Bunting, E. (1996). *The blue and the gray*. New York: Scholastic.
Hopkins, D. (1993). *Sweet Clara and the freedom quilt*. New York: Alfred A. Knopf.
Polacco, P. (1994). *Pink and Say*. New York: Philomel Books.
Ringold, F. (1992). *Aunt Harriet's Underground Railroad*. New York: Scholastic.
Turner, A. (1987). *Nettie's trip south*. New York: Macmillan.
Winter, J. (1988). *Follow the drinking gourd*. New York: Alfred A. Knopf.

Texts for Literature Discussions That Relate to World War II
(these are a combination of nonfiction and historical fiction young adult novels)

Choi, S.N. (1991). *Year of impossible goodbyes*. New York: Dell.
Coerr, E. (1977). *Sadako and the thousand paper cranes*. New York: Harper & Row.
Hess, K. (1992). *Letters from Rifka*. New York: Henry Holt.
Hoestlandt, J. (1993). *Star of fear, star of hope*. New York: Walker. (picture book)
Lowry, L. (1989). *Number the stars*. New York: Dell.
Perl, L., & Lazan, M.B. (1996). *Four perfect pebbles: A Holocaust story*. New York: Scholastic.
Pettit, J. (1993). *A place to hide. True stories of Holocaust rescue*. New York: Scholastic.
Reiss, J. (1972). *Upstairs room*. New York: Harper & Row.

Reflection Point 2.3

1. What types of books do you use with your students in your classroom? How do students respond to these books?

2. During the next several days, try to listen specifically to how students talk about what they are reading in your literacy class. Ask students what they think of the books they are reading. Are they animated and excited about what they are reading? Do their responses reveal a personal connection to their book?

3. What do your students' responses mean in relation to your decision to use literature discussion groups in your classroom?

After I selected the books, I gave students a brief synopsis of each book and then allowed them some time to browse through the selections. After browsing, they wrote their top three choices on an index card, and I used these cards to form the discussion groups. I often did not have enough books for everyone to receive their first choice but students always received one of their top three choices. I also reminded students that popular books would be offered again in future cycles, so they would have another opportunity to read those books if they were not placed in that group the first time around. I have found that this type of structured choice meets both my need for providing students with quality selections of literature, and students' need to have a voice in determining what they read. When I interviewed my students, they stated overwhelmingly that they wanted to have a choice in selecting their books and much preferred our system over simply having the teacher decide what they would read. Jackie stated this opinion very clearly:

> I like it better if we choose our own books because it's like, some books I don't like to read and some books I do. So if you gave me a book that I don't wanna read, then there's this other book that I really wanted to read, then that wouldn't be fair because it's like, if you've read the book already, and then you just give it to them, then they will know what's gonna happen so what's the use of reading it?

Allowing students choices is not without concerns. A common question I have heard numerous teachers ask is whether students will select appropriate books. This was seldom a problem in my classroom. Having books available at a variety of reading levels helped assure that there would be a match for each student's needs. By the fifth grade, most students had a good understanding of where they were in reading and what type of book would be too difficult for them. If a struggling reader did select a book that was technically too difficult for her, I always gave her a chance to at least try the book. Because I view reading as a process that is influenced by a reader's prior knowledge, experiences, and interests, I believe that a student can successfully read a book that might appear to be too difficult if she has sufficient prior knowledge of the topic and/or has a great deal of interest in reading the book. Also, because I believe that learning is a socially constructed process, I feel that students have the benefit of their group members to scaffold and support their reading and understanding of the text. I saw this happen in countless situations. A struggling reader would select a difficult book and then choose a partner to read with from her literature group. This peer would help the struggling reader deal with the difficult text, and could answer questions to clarify and facilitate the struggling peer's understanding of the book. Because of this, I was comfortable in allowing a struggling student to select a book that might be above her reading level. If you are not comfortable with it, however, the system of allowing students three choices while you determine the final groups still gives you the opportunity to place students with the book from their list that you feel is most closely matched to their ability level.

On the other end of the spectrum is the concern that able readers will select books that are too easy for them. Again, this was seldom an issue in my classroom, mainly because I worked hard to find titles that would appeal to students at all ability levels. When a capable reader did select a book that was below his level, however, I again allowed the student to read it because I believe that students can engage in meaningful discussions of literature even when reading a book below their ability level. (After all, my adult book group had a fabulous discussion of *The Giver* [Lowry, 1993] even though it probably would not match any of our actual reading levels.) Most often, I found that the higher ability student became bored with the easy book and selected a more difficult book for the next cycle. Again, if you are uncomfortable with allowing a student to read a book that is below his ability, you can place the student with the book from his three choices that most closely matches his reading level.

Reflection Point 2.4

1. How are texts selected in your classroom? Are students given choices about what they will read?

2. Ask your students how they feel about having a say in what they read. If this is something students would like, how might you think about incorporating some student choice into your literacy instruction?

Preparing the Discussion Groups for Independent Study

After forming the literature discussion groups based on student preferences, I gave the students their books and they met with their group to discuss why each of them had selected that book to read. During this initial meeting, students could hear other students' perspectives on the book and what they thought or hoped it would be about. The students also got a chance to decide how far they would read in the book before their first actual discussion meeting. I structured the week so that students met with their group for discussion on Tuesdays and Thursdays. Monday, Wednesday, and Friday were reserved for other literacy-related instruction and activities, and the students also had time to read their literature book. It is important to clarify that this reading time was separate from our Sustained Silent Reading (SSR) time. During SSR, students were allowed to read anything of their choice. During literature reading time, students were expected to read their literature book so that they could keep up with their group. Although I know many teachers who have literature discussions every day, I decided to have my groups meet only twice a week. Through observing students in their discussion groups, I discovered that many students—especially slow or struggling readers—often are not able to read enough of their book in a single day to have a sufficient amount of new information to bring to a discussion. This often results in a focus on superficial aspects of the text. You might want to experiment with the number of discussions per week in your classroom and see what works best for you and your students.

Once books have been picked, groups have been formed, and the students have decided how much of the book they will read in preparation for their first discussion meeting, it is time to think about how you might support their efforts to have a constructive, productive book discussion. In the next chapter, I present several of the methods I used to support my students' discussions. Before reading Chapter 3, take a few minutes to respond to the following Reflection Point questions.

Reflection Point 2.5

1. What types of literature discussions take place in your classroom? Are they whole-class, teacher-led discussions or small-group, student-led discussions?

2. What are you currently doing to support your students' discussion of books? Do your efforts result in the types of discussion you want? What concerns or questions do you have about "letting your students go" to conduct their own peer-led literature discussions?

Avoiding Round-Robin Discussions: The Need for Instructional Scaffolding

After observing the discussions today, I'm discouraged. Several groups appear to just be doing nothing and not getting the point of this at all. Two groups were already working on their end-of-the-book presentation ideas rather than discussing the book. The presentations have taken over, which makes me wonder if the students don't perceive the discussions as something necessary to do. It's just marking time until they're done with the book and can do their presentation. The Julie of the Wolves group was completely without any discussion. The students said they were confused by the book but did not ask each other any questions to help clarify their confusion. When I asked them what they had talked about in their discussion, they couldn't think of one issue. I tried to ask some questions to clarify their confusion and get some discussion going but they had no response and I didn't feel particularly effective in helping get a discussion going either. A student named Kristine offered the excuse that this wasn't really a book you could talk about—you needed to read it alone. I am very frustrated!

The above scenario is from my observation notes of Marcy's classroom and it is similar to many moments of frustration I have encountered during my years of working with literature discussion groups. I originally wondered if the students' lack of discussion was due to their not having a clear understanding of the purpose for these groups. However, when Marcy and I asked students to reflect on what the purpose of discussion was, most students were able to articulate an understanding that was consistent with our instructional goals (e.g., to help students become better readers, to hear other opinions about the book, to share ideas, etc.). Knowing this, I came to the conclusion that the students might need more explicit scaffolding to support their discussion attempts.

This chapter focuses on the three different types of scaffolding that I have used with literature discussion groups in an effort to move students closer to what Eeds and Wells (1989) call "grand conversations." I learned through trial and error that grand conversations do not occur on their own; they are the result of much hard work, planning, and scaffolding. But even the most carefully thought out scaffolding can result in less than optimal outcomes. Consequently, I will also discuss the possible pitfalls of the different types of scaffolding and illustrate how they have the potential to become crutches that inhibit grand conversations and result in superficial, round-robin discussions. Rather than reading this chapter as a "how to" manual for implementing literature discussion groups, I hope you will view it as an example of how much we can learn from our students when we keep them in sight and listen carefully to what their words and actions tell us. None of the ideas presented in this chapter are new, but I found that they were more effective when I modified and implemented them in response to what I saw and heard among my students.

Providing Discussion Topic Ideas

When students first experience literature discussion groups, many of them may share the uncertainty voiced by one of Marcy's students when he asked, "What are we supposed to do now?" I found that providing students with a list of possible discussion topics or questions was a helpful aid to facilitate talk. (See Appendix A for examples of discussion ideas.) Simply handing out a sheet of ideas, however, is not sufficient because students are likely to need explicit support in learning how to use the list of ideas to facilitate their discussion. I often relied on the class read-aloud book to model and demonstrate methods that could help students in their discussion. On the day that Marcy and I handed out the list of discussion ideas, we went through each idea and clarified any questions students had about what each one meant; we then generated an example from our read-aloud book to illustrate each idea. While reading the read-aloud book, I stopped and demonstrated how I might answer a question from the discussion list. I then asked students how they might answer the question, thus giving them an example of how to facilitate a discussion among group members. I usually allowed students free choice in deciding which questions they wanted to focus on in their discussion, but if you would like to add more structure to your groups you can direct students to particular questions that match your instructional goal or purpose. For example, you could instruct students to address the question of where the story takes place; this will emphasize the literary element of setting and draw students' attention to how the setting influences the story.

The example that follows shows a group discussion that occurred in Marcy's classroom the day after she and I gave students the list of ideas and demonstrated how to use it. This discussion is not exactly my notion of a grand conversation, but it provides a general idea of where students are likely to be in their beginning efforts to use this type of scaffolding. The group was reading the self-selected book, *The Great Gilly Hopkins* (Paterson, 1978).

Michael:	OK. Let's do #1 (on the list of ideas): "Relate the book to your own experience." Does anyone have a time when they really miss their mom or anything? I know I have.
Jessie:	I can relate to missing my mom (tells story of going on vacation with her dad).
Michael:	I can relate (tells story of missing his mom).
Jessie:	I think we should do #4 and #3 next.
Michael:	I think we should do #12—what people/places look like. Let's take Agnes Stokes. She's a fairly—
Keely:	She wants to be Gilly's friend but Gilly don't want her to be her friend.
Michael:	Yeah. We know that she's shorter than Gilly, she has long red hair, she has a mouth problem, a big mouth problem.
Jessie:	And she like wants to hang around Gilly a lot.
Michael:	And they both like bubble gum.

As the concept of scaffolding suggests, the goal is to provide explicit support in the initial stages of learning a new skill or concept and then to gradually wean students away from the external support as they become more able to engage in the skill independently. My goal in giving students a list of discussion ideas was for them to eventually reach a point at which they no longer needed the list of topics to help guide their discussions. The next example focuses on a different discussion group a month after Marcy and I first introduced the idea list. The students were reading *How to Get Fabulously Rich* by Thomas Rockwell (1991). The group still uses many of the ideas from the original list, however, they are no longer holding the list in front of them and reading the items off one-by-one to structure their discussion. Rather, they use the ideas in a much more fluid, natural way to guide their discussion. It is important to consider that this progression did not happen overnight, nor did it happen with every group. My purpose in presenting these two examples is to illustrate how this scaffolding method might look over time with your own students, and to show how they might progress given more practice and experience in using the list in their discussion groups.

Michael:	Anybody got any predictions?
Pete:	I think he gets all that money and is gonna do something weird with it.
Michael:	I think he's gonna cause a big conflict between his friends.
Pete:	Like a riot or something.
Brad:	I think he might start bragging 'cuz he has all the money.
Pete:	And he won't have any friends.
Michael:	And remember his mom, or whoever he's living with, said, (in a sarcastic voice and making a face), "use it for college, use it for college."
Brad:	I'd put half in my bank account.
Michael:	I'd put like $10,000 in. How much does college cost?
Brad:	Wasn't that his friend who was saying that? Wait, first we have to know how much he has, how much he won.
Michael:	$410,000.
Pete:	See, that ain't all that much. In the lottery they're like giving away 42 million dollars and stuff. Just a million would be enough for me.

Brad:	I'd put $300,000 in my bank account.
Michael:	Is there any main character who's sort of like keeping the tempo going?
Pete:	There's likely hardly anybody else in there, really.
Michael:	I know. This is a weird book.
Brad:	All they talk about is lottery and his money.
Michael:	We've read over half the book so far and nothing exciting.
Jalil:	No one's got killed or nothing.
Michael:	I know. He hasn't gotten into trouble.
Pete:	It's all on the same thing.
Brad:	He's not even going away or anything when his parents die.
Jalil:	Maybe they should put in something exciting like he gets arrested.
Pete:	Yeah! Like he goes to jail and then he has to use all his money to get freed out.
Brad:	If I won the lottery I'd probably buy a house.
Michael:	I know, I'd buy a house. I'd buy a big house.
Pete:	Couple of cars!
Brad:	How would you though? You don't have your parents. You have to have your parents to sign all the papers.
Michael:	Well, the people that he lives with.
Brad:	I'd buy two houses, one to live in the summer. I'd buy a maid. Video games.
Pete:	I'd buy a whole bunch of stuff. I'd make my own fishing pond and stock it up with as many fish as I could.
Michael:	Use money as bait (laughing)! Oh, it's a big one (pretending to reel in fish).
Pete:	It's a money fish!
Jalil:	All they talk about is money, lottery, money, lottery.
Michael:	He's created no suspense, no tension.
Brad:	Oh, I know one. Wouldn't they put him in a foster home or with his grandma or something?
Pete:	Yeah.
Michael:	You know what he should have done to create suspense, they should have had the batteries run out on his radio so he couldn't get the final lottery numbers. That'd be cool.

Pete: I know. Or right when he gets the money, somebody tries to shoot him but he misses so he starts running and he like disturbs all the peace so he has to go to jail and that one lady has to bail him out with all the money he just won so then there'd be no more money left.

Reflection Point 3.1

1. Using the list provided in Appendix A and your own instructional purpose, put together a discussion list to use with your own students. Explain the list and provide examples of its use to students. If you are currently using literature discussion groups, ask your students to use the list in their discussion this week. If you are not using literature discussion groups, use your class read-aloud book and have students divide into groups to discuss it. Depending on your comfort level, either allow students free choice in what items they will discuss, or direct students to focus on a few specific items.

2. Select one group to observe this week and take notes as you listen to their discussion. How are they using the list? Does it facilitate their discussion? In what ways?

3. Wait a week and observe this same group (or a different group if your students do not stay in the same groups). How are they using the list now? Is it facilitating their discussion? Do you notice any changes in their conversation from last week?

As you reflect on your response to the previous Reflection Point you will want to keep in mind that a week may not be a sufficient amount of time to notice a substantial change. However, you may begin to see subtle changes in how students use the discussion list and its possibilities for facilitating a constructive discussion.

Literature Response Logs

Karen:	How do you feel about writing in your response log?
Mimi:	I don't like it because I don't like to write.
Mia:	Boring. I don't like to. We have to write in complete sentences.
Jane:	Yeah. You have to write in complete sentences and you can't just have one or two sentences, you have to have like at least a half a page or something.
Alicia:	I hate writing in them. It's like so hard because there's probably nothing I can think of to write. Usually I put, "I like this book but I wish it had maps in it," or other stuff I want in it. Then I put my opinion of it and back it up. I try to do that for every chapter but it's just hard.
Karen:	Does writing in your lit log help your discussion?
Jonathan:	No.
Mimi:	No.
Karen:	Why not?
Jonathan:	Well, you already know what you wrote and you just talk about it.
Mimi:	Because we already know what we're going to say; why do you have to write it down?

When I heard these sentiments being voiced by Clay and Roxanne's students, I was surprised and curious. In my initial reading and learning about literature discussion groups, it seemed as if literature response logs were a ubiquitous aspect of these groups. All the research I had read advocated their use and talked about how the logs supported student discussions and facilitated student response to and understanding of their books (Hancock, 1993; Kelly & Farnan, 1991; Martinez, Roser, Hoffman, & Battle, 1992). Why then did these students think so negatively about their response logs—especially because three of the students (Mia, Alicia, and Jane) were excellent readers and writers who consistently engaged in thoughtful discussions of their books? As I continued to listen to the students, I learned some valuable lessons about how students perceive response logs and how they might actually detract from, rather than support, our efforts to engage students in discussions of literature. The students' insights helped me to reconsider the role of response logs and raised some interesting questions regarding their use in facilitating discussion.

The students in Clay and Roxanne's classroom had free choice as to what they wrote in their literature logs, but as the earlier remarks suggest there were clear expectations regarding the form and length of their comments. Students were to write in complete sentences, and they were expected to write more than a couple of sentences for each entry. I can understand the length requirement because Clay and Roxanne wanted students to use their logs as places to really engage with what they were reading and respond in meaningful ways to their book. I wonder, though, if the length requirement was partially influenced by the examples of response log entries that are regularly found in research journal articles. These sample entries are usually lengthy, thoughtful, and meaningful, and definitely show the power that response logs can have. However, they also portray a possibly unrealistic expectation that all students will write about their books in this way. Also contributing to the expectations about the form and length of log entries was the fact that Clay and Roxanne periodically collected the literature logs and graded them. I think many teachers use response logs as a form of assessment and the appeal of doing so is obvious—it is a clear way to see how students are responding to their books. Teachers cannot be in every discussion group at every moment to hear what students say about the book, but they can see what students have written each time. In fact, students viewed the response logs as a type of "check up" on them. Alicia commented that the purpose of the response logs was not to help her group have a meaningful discussion, but rather "so [the teachers] will know you're not just always just kind of fake reading."

These students' responses emphasize how important it is for us to be clear about our purpose for using literature response logs. If our purpose is to help students respond to their book and support their discussions, do complete sentences and length really matter? If response logs are to be a "repository for wanderings and wonderings, speculations, questionings...a place to explore thoughts, discover reactions, let the mind ramble...a place to make room for the unexpected" (Flitterman-King, 1988, p. 5), should length and format be a concern? Should students be expected to worry about spelling at the same time they are wondering about, reacting to, and exploring their book? Are we not possibly hindering their ability to respond in meaningful, personal ways when we also ask them to attend to the conventions of writing in their response logs? These are the types of questions we must ask ourselves when using this activity with our students. If we are not clear about our purpose—and if students' perceptions of why they are writing in logs are not consistent with our purpose—then response logs have the potential to become merely another form of comprehension-check worksheet rather than a way to help students respond to literature.

Reflection Point 3.2

1. Take a few minutes to write out your purpose for using literature response logs with your students. Write a description of how you actually implement response logs in your classroom. Look for connections between your responses to these two instructions. Are your goals and purposes reflected in how you use response logs in your classroom?

2. Next, ask a few of your students what their thoughts are regarding their response logs—how they feel about them and what they think is the purpose for writing in them. Are their perceptions consistent with your instructional purpose? If there are discrepancies, what changes might you make so that your goals are more clearly reflected in how you use response logs with your students?

This discussion is not meant to discourage the use of literature response logs; rather, my goal is to highlight some of the roadblocks we may encounter if we are not thoughtful about why and how we use them. The insights provided by Clay and Roxanne's students definitely influenced how Marcy and I used response logs in her classroom. We did not have grammar or spelling expectations for the students because we wanted their full mental energy to be spent on getting their thoughts down on paper. We also did not have length requirements because our purpose in using the logs was to support students' discussions, and we believed that simply jotting down short notes or phrases could be sufficient to jog a student's memory for what she wanted to discuss with her group. We were more concerned with what students actually talked about in their discussions than how much they wrote in their response log. This is an important distinction because an alternative use of response logs is for students to read and respond in writing to each other's logs (often called dialogue journals), or for the teacher and student to dialogue in the response log. In this type of framework the discussion occurs in writing, and the form and length of the response take on more importance because someone else will have to be able to read and interpret it. Dialogue journals were not used as a response format in my classroom, but they represent a viable alternative to discussion groups. If you would like more information on how to use them, refer to the resources in Box 3.1.

Even if students are not given format and length requirements, they are still likely to need support in learning how to use response logs to facilitate their discussion. Marcy and I did this through demonstrations related to the read-aloud book and connected with the discussion idea list. During read-aloud we would periodically stop and model writing in our response logs for students, making sure to identify which item on the list

---

Box 3.1
Resources for Using Dialogue Journals

Beach, R., & Anson, C. (1993). Using peer-dialogue journals to foster response. In G.E. Newell & R.K. Durst (Eds.), *Exploring texts: The role of discussion and writing in the teaching and learning of literature* (pp. 191–210). Norwood, MA: Christopher-Gordon.

Farest, C., & Miller, C. (1993). Children's insights into literature: Using dialogue journals to invite literary response. In D.J. Leu & C.K. Kinzer (Eds.), *Examining central issues in literacy research, theory, and practice: Forty-second yearbook of the National Reading Conference* (pp. 271–278). Chicago: National Reading Conference.

Harste, J.C., Short, K., & Burke, C. (1988). *Creating classrooms for authors.* Portsmouth, NH: Heinemann.

Readence, J.E., Bean, T.W., & Baldwin, R.S. (1998). *Content area literacy: An integrated approach* (6th ed.). Dubuque, IA: Kendall/Hunt.

Tierney, R., Readence, J.E., & Dishner, E. (1995). *Reading strategies and practices: A compendium.* Boston: Allyn & Bacon.

our response related to best. For example, when I read *Words By Heart*, (Sebestyen, 1979) to the class, I paused at the part where the main character, Lena, "borrowed" a book from her employer because she loved reading and did not have any books of her own. I wrote the following on the board as an example of my response log:

> This part reminds me of when I picked all the pussy willows off of my elderly neighbor's bush because I thought they were so soft and I wanted them all to myself. I had never stolen anything in my entire life before. I felt guilty, but not guilty enough to stop. My mom made me go and apologize when she found out what I did. I wonder if Lena's father will make her return the book and apologize?

We then discussed how this was an example of relating the book to personal experience, and I asked if anyone else had had a similar experience in order to model using response log entries to generate discussion.

Marcy and I shared our responses throughout the read-aloud sessions, and students told us that it helped them to get an idea of the kinds of things they could write about in their logs. However, we still found a wide variation in the type and quality of the students' written responses. Consider the following examples:

> These two chapters were the best ever. (Damon, *Sharing Susan*)

> I like the book so far. The dog is cute. (Amy, *Strider*)

> Right now I wouldn't want to be in his position now because he's having bad luck. I hope he finds his mother. (Tim, *Monkey Island*)

> I hope Shiloh does get better. If I were Shiloh I think I would try to make Marty like me so I could stay with him. Shiloh reminds me of my cat. My cat got hurt by another animal and he has a bad wound on his head but it still hasn't healed. (Hannah, *Shiloh*)

> If I were Cracker, I would still go over to Alma's house once in awhile to check on her. I don't think I would have told my father about Alma. I wonder why Alma and Cracker didn't know that leeches were on their ankles. (Kari, *Cracker Jackson*)

> I love this book it is so interesting. I am waiting for when she has to meet her real mom and dad. I would be anxious to meet them. But I would also be really scared to meet them too because these are people I have

never ever met before. It's like meeting a total stranger and then have the people you thought were your parents say these are your real parents. I seriously would freak out. P.S. I would never shave my eyebrows. (Noelia, *Sharing Susan*)

Student responses varied from Damon's and Amy's unsupported, superficial comments to entries in which students wrote emotional responses to the book, related the book to personal experience, and discussed what they would do if they were in a character's place. Because Marcy and I viewed the response logs as a springboard to discussion, rather than a definitive indication of a student's ability to respond to and interact with the book, these differences were not problematic to us. If a student such as Damon did not write extensively in his response log, we could use our observation of his discussion group to see whether he understood and interacted with his book.

With support and modeling of response log entries, Marcy's students grew in their ability to use this tool to facilitate their discussions. In the following example, the group was reading Betsy Byars's *Cracker Jackson* (1985). Note how students used their response logs as springboards for discussion.

Amy: (reading her log)"I want to know what 'keep away Cracker or he'll hurt you' means."

Noelia: Like, because of Billy Ray. He wanted to hurt him so she tried to keep Cracker away because if you read more in the book, it said that he, it was OK at first when she was baby-sitting but now that she doesn't have to baby-sit anymore, I think he's annoying to Billy.

Amy: I think the chapters we read today were really freaky. I was scared out of my wits!

Jessie: OK, I'll go next. I wrote,"I think Alma is lying about Billy Ray because if you walked into a door, I don't think you'd get a black eye. Because I walk into doors all the time (giggle) at night—"

Noelia: So do I!

Amy: I just hurt my nose.

Jessie: Yeah, I just hurt my nose, or like right here (points to side of face).

Noelia:	I don't see why 'cause your nose would probably hit the door more instead of your eyes.
Amy:	Unless you're walking sideways. 'Cause your eyes are farther back.
Jessie:	Or, you could hit your forehead because I do that all the time when I wake up in the morning and no lights are on or nothing or I have to go to the bathroom, I just run into the door.
Noelia:	But I still think that Cracker knows that Billy Ray [gave her the black eye].
Jessie:	And I wrote, if she is like lying, why would she cover up for Billy Ray? That's what I want to know.
Kari:	'Cause you'd think she'd want to turn him in or something (general nods of agreement).
Noclia:	But maybe she's scared—
Amy:	And not tell Billy Ray she told.
Noelia:	But she might be scared though that—
Amy:	—he'll do something.
Noelia:	If he found out, she would get beaten even more.
Amy:	Yeah.
Jessie:	But she might, if the cops came, I'm just saying if they did, while he's at his job, Alma could stay at Cracker's house.
Noelia:	I think Billy Ray would find out though. I think that'd be the first place he'd look.
Amy:	Yeah.
Jessie:	And then they could go arrest Billy Ray.
Amy:	But then if Billy Ray gets out, maybe the next day 'cause he lies, and then he can come back and get—
Noelia:	Yeah, 'cause they don't actually have proof that Billy Ray did it to her.
Jessie:	Yeah, 'cause they might believe that she walked into a door, but that's pretty kind of—
Amy:	—pretty obvious that they would, look at the door and see if there's a dent or something.
Jessie:	Yeah, 'cause your eyes are further back in your head than like, you can break your nose—

Amy:	You have to get punched pretty darn hard to get a black eye.
Jessie:	Yeah, if I did this to myself (hits herself in face), I won't get a black eye.
Noelia:	I've gotten hit in the eye with a football going fast and it didn't give me a black eye.
Jessie:	Courtney yesterday got hit with a football and her eye didn't turn black or anything, while I was at her house, it just got all red.
Noelia:	(reading her log) "I would call the police on Billy Ray but for sure I wouldn't go to the house like Cracker did. And I would still call and make sure Alma's OK because Billy Ray can't do anything over the phone."
Jessie:	Yeah, but he could come over though.
Amy:	Yeah, and I think she should just get out of the house and like go to a hotel or something.
Noelia:	She also has a baby though, too.
Jessie:	Yeah, baby Nicole.
Noelia:	Still the baby's suffering, too.
Amy:	It's watching them fight. It's gonna teach that baby to beat up too, you know!
Jessie:	But if you read this (back cover of book), it says that there's wife battering and child abuse so I think like something's going to happen to baby Nicole (nods of agreement).
Kari:	(reading her log) "I wonder why Cracker Jackson's mother didn't want Alma calling him Cracker? Why did she just write in her letter that he should keep away? Why wouldn't Alma's husband like it when Cracker came over? What does he have to hide?"

The girls continued to discuss the book, and Kari's response log entry sparked another substantial amount of discussion. In this example, the girls' response log entries were only a few sentences long, but they used them effectively to generate a discussion that was meaningful, related to their personal experiences, and also extended their understanding of the text. Observing this type of discussion helped Marcy and I feel more comfortable about our lack of length requirement. We could see that students were using their two- or three-sentence response logs as effective spring-boards to thoughtful, productive discussions.

If you would like additional structural guidelines for using response logs, the sources in Box 3.2 relate to research conducted with these logs and offer suggestions for how to use them in connection to literature discussion groups.

Box 3.2
Resources for Using Literature Response Logs

Hancock, M. (1993). Exploring and extending personal response through literature journals. *The Reading Teacher, 46*, 466–474.

Kelly, P., & Farnan, N. (1991). Promoting critical thinking through response logs: A reader-response approach with fourth graders. In J. Zutell & S. McCormick (Eds.), *Learner factors/teacher factors: Issues in literacy research and instruction: Fortieth Yearbook of the National Reading Conference* (pp. 277–284). Chicago: National Reading Conference.

Martinez, M., Roser, N., Hoffman, J., & Battle, J. (1992). Fostering better book discussions through response logs and a response framework: A case description. In C.K. Kinzer & D.J. Leu (Eds.), *Literacy research, theory, and practice: Views from many perspectives: Forty-first Yearbook of the National Reading Conference* (pp. 303–311). Chicago: National Reading Conference.

Routman, R. (1994). *Invitations: Changing as teachers and learners K–12*. Portsmouth, NH: Heinemann.

Wollman-Bonilla, J., & Werchadlo, B. (1995). Literature response journals in a first-grade classroom. *Language Arts, 72*(8), 562–570.

Do I Have to Respond to My Students' Response Logs?

I would like to address briefly the issue of teachers responding to their students' response logs, because this has been a dilemma for me. Many researchers advocate the idea that teachers should respond to what their students write in their logs. Hancock (1993) states that redirecting and expanding students' responses, as well as inspiring deeper thinking, is best accomplished through teacher comments in students' logs. Although I agree with this idea in theory, in practice I have found it very difficult. The type of teacher response required to expand a student's response or inspire deeper thinking is often very time consuming to write. I constantly struggled to find the time to write such responses in each student's log on a regular basis.

Time was an issue for Marcy too, so when she read students' logs, she usually wrote brief comments such as, "I felt the same way, Why did you think that? I had the same question," and often wrote no comments at all. We found that students did not seem to miss a written response in their logs. I think this was largely due to the fact that the students received responses to what they had written when they shared and talked about their comments in their discussion group. Consistent with our social constructivist beliefs, we discovered that students were able to create a zone of proximal development in their discussion groups by being each other's more capable peer (Vygotsky, 1978). Students were very competent at providing feedback that redirected and expanded their classmates' responses and encouraged deeper thinking as a result of the multiple perspectives and ideas offered by their peers. They did not need to rely only on the teacher to provide this type of feedback. The earlier example from the *Cracker Jackson* group illustrates how student discussion served the same purpose as a teacher's written response and provided students with a richer opportunity to explore and expand their response to the book than anything Marcy or I could have written to them.

Grappling With Round-Robin Response Logs

> I'm discouraged again. The kids just don't seem to be getting this whole discussion thing. I sat in with the *Monkey Island* group today and even though they had all written something in their log, it was like pulling teeth. They still do the old "everybody round-robin read their log" and then they don't know what to do next. There's no elaboration or response to the log entries. (excerpt from Karen's observation journal)

Not all student discussions were as thoughtful as that of the *Cracker Jackson* group, nor did students' response logs always serve as a springboard for discussion. Throughout the year, Marcy and I observed groups that used response logs as round-robin discussion tools where each student read his log and that constituted the discussion. This was a consistent source of frustration for us because we knew the students were capable of more. I had observed the same students in the *Monkey Island* group engage in thoughtful, animated, issue-delving discussions in previous groups. Why did the same students exhibit such different behaviors in different groups? One possible explanation is simply the book being read. When students read a book that really interested them, we did not observe round-robin discussion. Another possibility is the composition of the group, a matter that will be explored further in Chapter 6. Aside from these concerns, however, Marcy and I wondered what we could do to better support students in their current discussion groups, moving them from round-robin response log sharing to grand conversations.

In looking at the students' response logs and listening to their discussions, it was clear that they related their books to personal experiences and often put themselves in the place of a character. This is one approach to generating a response. Another way—one that seemed absent from many response logs—is the strategy of students raising questions as they read the book. These questions can then be posed to the group and used to facilitate discussion, explore multiple interpretations, and extend understanding of the text. The students initially did not write many questions in their response logs, because often this was viewed as the teacher's job. The traditional discussion format used in many classrooms consists of the teacher asking questions and the students answering them. Because many of Marcy's students had a lot of experience with traditional discussions, but little experience in leading their own discussions, we thought it likely that they were not accustomed to asking questions about what they read. Consequently, we decided to do a strategy lesson on Question-Answer-Relationships (QARs) (Raphael, 1986) and "I wonder" statements (Mitchell-Pierce, 1998) as a way to expand the types of responses that students wrote in their logs.

Asking Genuine, Thought-Provoking Questions

Raphael's (1986) system of QARs focuses on three different types of questions: Right There, Think and Search, and On My Own. Right There questions have the answers stated explicitly in the text—they are "right there" on the page. Think and Search questions are similar to inferential questions. The author provides clues to answer the question, but the reader has to find the clues, put them together, and think about how to use them to answer the question. On My Own questions are those that relate the text to a student's own experience (e.g., Have you ever felt that way?). For the purpose of stimulating discussion, Think and Search and On My Own questions are the most helpful, so our strategy lesson focused on these two types of questions. In the following journal entry I describe a QAR lesson.

> After read aloud, I did the strategy lesson today on questioning. I first went over the 3 types of questioning (Raphael's system) on the overhead and gave examples of each from the read-aloud book. Then I read the book *Crow Boy* (Yashima, 1955) and asked them to work together in their seating groups to generate all the questions they could think of about the book. At first it was slow going and most groups were unsure about what to do. There were a lot of blank sheets for a few minutes and lots of uncertain looks. After a few minutes, I had them volunteer their questions and put them all on the board. It was great! They actually were eager to share and had numerous hands up at once. Their questions were very thoughtful too. I was quite impressed for the first go-around. Of course there were some of the traditional comprehension-check questions but they were definitely in the minority. Questions included the following:
>
>> Where did Chibi come from?
>>
>> Why didn't the author mention his mom or dad?
>>
>> How did he manage 6 years with no friends?
>>
>> Why was Chibi so small?
>>
>> How did he feel about being called Chibi?
>>
>> Why was he called Crow Boy?
>>
>> Is Chibi a name in a different language?
>>
>> What was his real name?
>>
>> Where did the story take place?
>>
>> Could the teacher understand his writing?
>>
>> How did he learn to imitate crows?
>>
>> Why were the students mean to Chibi?
>>
>> Why did he hide under the school?
>
> As our conversation continued, I literally had the entire board filled with questions and students had more but I ran out of room. I think they were rather surprised too. I then talked about how these questions could help us if we were to have a discussion group on this book and how writing questions can be one way of helping them in their literature discussion groups. We then tried to classify some of their questions using Raphael's system. They were able to identify some Right There questions but there weren't very many of those (yea!). Also, when they classified "Could the teacher understand his writing?" as a Right There question, Amy asked, "How did he do his schoolwork if the teacher couldn't understand his writing?" This was an example of a great spin-off question from a literal, Right There question. Several students made comments about her ques-

tion and I explained how that was a great example of how one person's question can often lead to other questions and before you know it, you have plenty to talk about. Students then identified several Think and Search questions and recognized that most of their questions were that type. There were no On My Own questions but that's OK since they're already asking those types of questions in their logs and discussions.

The next day I modeled "I wonder" statements (Mitchell-Pierce, 1998) using the read-aloud book *Words By Heart* (Sebestyen, 1979). "I wonder" statements are questions that reflect genuine issues or topics that a reader can discuss with other group members, using the phrase "I wonder" to begin the question. After reading a portion of the text, I wrote the following "I wonder" statements on the board and asked students how these statements could lead to a discussion:

I wonder what Papa saw inside Mr. Haney when he stopped and looked inside him?

I wonder what Papa would see inside me if he looked inside me?

I wonder where Mr. Haney is going?

I wonder what Papa meant when he said to Lena, "When are you going to master yourself?"

I asked students to generate their own "I wonder" statements about the read-aloud book, and I recorded them on the board. To help demonstrate how these statements could facilitate discussion, I asked each seating group (students' desks were arranged in groups of four) to select one or two "I wonder" statements and discuss them among themselves. We then shared the individual groups' responses to the statements with the whole class.

After the lesson, I told students that everyone would be responsible for writing at least one question in their response log before the next discussion. The students' subsequent response logs and discussions reflected the influence of the questioning lesson. The group reading *The Great Gilly Hopkins* (Paterson, 1978) had been struggling from the beginning. The students were angry and frustrated with each other and their discussions were often a fine line away from being arguments. When I observed them the day after the questioning lesson, their interactions had changed significantly. They said unanimously that the discussion was going much better and that having the questions really helped them. Jessie responded exuberantly, "This is the first time we knew what to talk about so we didn't just sit there and be bored or get into fights." Michael added, "We decided that we're going to write questions every time from now on." I later read their response logs to see what questions they had written to facilitate their discussion and whether they continued to write questions. Here's a sampling of what I found:

I wonder if Gilly will ever think of Trotter's boy as a friend and not try to be better than him?

I wonder if Gilly will ever like her new school?

I wonder if Gilly will ever see her mom again or try to run away?

Since Gilly is trying to get good grades to pass other students, will she start to like school?

What made Gilly change her attitude?

Michael

Why was W.E. scared when Gilly tried to pat him on the back when he was choking?

Did Gilly think Miss Harris hated the card? Did she?

Jessie

What was Gilly like to her parents?

What is Gilly going to act like in school?

Why is Gilly acting so nice and cleaning the house?

Keely

Why did the author use the term "bloody genius"?

Why were the prices so low?

I wonder if Gilly will find a way to stay with her mom?

I wonder if Gilly will start to like her grandma's house?

Stan

Reflection Point 3.3

1. Tape record one of your student discussion groups. While listening to their discussion, pay particular attention to the types of questions students raise. Also look at their literature logs for questions they had while reading. How are they using their questions to facilitate their discussion?

2. If you feel your students might benefit from a strategy lesson on questioning or from some explicit modeling of "I wonder" statements, try implementing such a lesson with your class.

3. Record the discussion group after your lesson and again listen to the types of questions students bring to their discussion and how they use them. Do you notice any differences in how your students use questions or "I wonder" statements in their discussions after your strategy lesson?

Who Decides What Is a Genuine Question?

I have often listened to my students' discussions and cringed at what I initially considered to be superficial conversations. Upon further reflection, however, I have come to see that my agenda of creating "grand conversations" can sometimes limit my ability to really hear what my students are talking about. Vivian Paley (1986), a kindergarten teacher, researcher, and writer, advises that, "the first order of reality in the classroom is the student's point of view" (p. 127). Her advice reminds me of the importance of valuing and validating my students' questions, discussions, and realities, even when they do not match my notion of thought-provoking questions, grand conversations, or meaningful realities. In the transcript examples that follow, I show how my students' discussions pushed me to reconsider my egocentric notion of what constitutes a meaningful discussion question or thoughtful conversation.

Similar to the earlier dilemma regarding round-robin literature logs, I often was frustrated by the students' use of round-robin questioning. When Marcy and I encouraged students to ask questions in their discussions, we sometimes heard rote renditions of the types of "teacher questions" that appeared on the discussion topic lists we distributed to the students. For example, consider the following discussion from the group reading *The Face on the Milk Carton* (Cooney, 1991):

Ethan:	What do you predict will happen?
Hannah:	I think she'll find her real parents.
Jalil:	I think her parents will find her.

Keely:	She'll never get her driver's license.
Ethan:	I think she'll search for her parents and she'll get closer and closer to them.
Stefan:	I think she might see her real parents but she won't know it's them but by the end of the story she'll find out they weren't her real parents.
Ethan:	OK, let's go to the next one—critique the book.

In this example, you can hear Ethan assuming the teacher's role and asking a generic prediction question while the rest of his group responds in round-robin fashion. This is similar to many teacher-led discussions that masquerade as gentle inquisitions (Eeds & Wells, 1984). None of the responses are discussed further, and there is no elaboration or questioning of each other's opinions by the group members. They merely answer the question and move on. After listening to several discussion groups that used "teacher" questions in this way, I began to get somewhat frustrated with the students. Then the *Sharing Susan* group reminded me that what appears to be a generic, non–discussion-generating question, can actually lead to a substantive discussion.

Joseph:	What do you guys think will happen at the end of the book?
Noelia:	Like, she'll stay with her birth parents, or, not her birth parents, but the parents who raised her.
Joseph:	That's what I thought. I thought that these parents would realize that she's not [indecipherable]. I think there's two ways that it could happen.
Noelia:	But would you think that she wasn't their daughter? 'Cause they look so much alike.
Kaitlyn:	I know. Doesn't she have to go with these people?
Damon:	She don't have to.
Daria:	She don't have to until she's 19 years old and so she can choose who she wants to stay with.
Joseph:	I think these two, the parents who gave birth, they're gonna realize that Susan, the other parents know what they're doing.
Daria:	Yeah.
Joseph:	Susan likes them better. They have good rules and that's

one way I think that she'll stay with the parents who raised her. The second way is I think they'll just keep sharing and she'll get to know these parents too.

Damon: I think that she'll like, stay with the parents who raised her and then like on holidays, like the parents that gave birth to her might come over there and stuff.

Joseph: I think they could come over more often.

Noelia: I think they're gonna split up like Christmas. Like, one year she'll come to the birth parents—

Joseph: Yeah. I think everybody should go to the house, they should switch houses. Everybody should go to the same house.

Daria: They should just switch off houses.

Noelia: What if they have a fight though?

Daria: They're not gonna fight. You see how nice they're being to these parents and these parents are being nice to them.

Noelia: They're not being nice. The birth parents are kind of rude I'd like to say. That's her choice if she wants to drink cappuccino. Who in the world really cares if she wants to drink coffee?

Daria: Oh yeah. (in sarcastic voice imitating parents) "Oh, she's too young to drink some cappuccino."

Joseph: Yeah, I know but they didn't say it like that.

Noelia: They gave her a weird look.

Joseph: How do you know? They don't show a picture?

Daria: They said it in the book.

Noelia: That's true. It said it in the book that they looked at her.

Joseph: But they don't know the rules either.

This discussion was initiated by Joseph asking a generic prediction question, but rather than answer in round-robin fashion, this group took off and explored various answers—revealing the multiple interpretations the students had of the book. Listening to this group reminded me that even though my students may not ask the types of thought-provoking, discussion-generating questions that were modeled in our questioning minilesson (or write them in their literature logs), they can still use generic questions to stimulate meaningful discussion. I realize this may sound somewhat contradictory to my discussion of questioning and the questioning minilesson presented earlier, but I am raising this issue to illustrate that we should be cautious in how we evaluate what may appear to be mundane or not particularly thoughtful questions. Although we may model thought-provoking questions, and students may use such questions to generate thoughtful discussions, they are not the only types of questions that provide students with entry into the world of meaningful discussions. As Michelle Commeyras (1994) reminds us, good discussion questions are those that students *want* to discuss—not those we think they *should* discuss.

Another dilemma I often faced was that of letting my "teacher persona" intrepret students' discussions as superficial. In the following transcript the girls are discussing the book *Homecoming* (Voigt, 1981).

Nicole:	Hey, don't you think Will and Claire are going to get married? They're always traveling everywhere.
All students:	No.
Heather:	Claire is already married.
Nicole:	No she isn't.
Vivian:	Will and Dicey should get married.
Junie:	Or Stuart and Windy should get married.
Alison:	They're two boys! (general ooohs, laughing).
Junie:	I mean Dicey. Windy and Stuart should get married to Dicey.
Alison:	I think Will was like a dad to them.
Junie:	Yeah, he buys her food, lets her stay.
Alison:	And she kisses him on the cheek and stuff.
Nicole:	I know. She goes up there and hugs him and gives him a big' ol kiss.
Vivian:	You know who I think should get married? Dicey and Jerry.
Alison:	He's like, "Have you ever (indecipherable) before? and how old are you?" I think he likes Dicey.

(All students respond at once, general agreement.)

Vivian:	But she's too young, remember that?
Nicole:	She should have lied and said she was 15.
Alison:	56.

Vivian:	Why?
Missy:	So you could be boyfriend and girlfriend.
Junie:	I wouldn't want to marry Jerry. He's ugly. I wanted her to marry Will.
Missy:	Really?
Junie:	He had a nice personality, except he was a little too old.

When I first listened to this conversation, I was disappointed that the girls focused on issues of dating and marriage partners rather than all the "meaty" issues raised in the book. Again, keeping Vivian Paley's advice in mind helped provide an alternative way to interpret the girls' discussion. I wanted them to address issues in the book such as homelessness, abandonment, searching for parents, and assuming adult responsibilities as a child, but that was not the reality for these girls. Their reality consisted of being 10- and 11-year-old girls who were on the fringe of entering the world of boy-girl relationships. They were intensely curious about things such as boys, looks, hair, and dating. Is it any wonder that these interests influenced how they read the book and found their way into the girls' discussions?

By refocusing my view of this type of discussion, I was able to see that it represented another example of my beliefs in practice. I believe that students' prior knowledge and interests influence the meaning they construct of what they read, and these girls helped me see that this was exactly what was happening. Rather than being simplistic or shallow, their discussion represented their reality and revealed how that reality interacted with the book to create a relevant meaning for them. It might not have matched my notion of what was important in the book, but part of the reason for using literature discussion groups is to allow students the opportunity to discuss issues that are relevant and interesting to *them*, not to the teacher. Again, I realize this may sound contradictory to my advocacy of grand conversations. However, I share this example to illustrate the need for us to broaden our notion of what constitutes a grand conversation to include students' perspectives, lives, and realities. This increases the likelihood that we will indeed keep our students in sight and make their perspectives the first order of reality in our classrooms.

Reflection Point 3.4

1. Revisit the responses you recorded for Reflection Point 3.3. Were there questions raised by your students that you felt were either superficial or generic?

2. How might you refocus your perception to look at these questions and discussions through the perspective of the students' reality? How might what you know about your students as individuals help provide an alternate way for you to interpret their conversations?

Critical Questions—Critical Literacy

I'd like to briefly address the issue of using critical questions as a way to facilitate critical literacy (Cherland & Edelsky, 1993; Davies, 1993; Simpson, 1996). Proponents of critical literacy claim that students should be taught that stories are not reflections of reality, but rather are selective versions of it (Simpson, 1996). Critical literacy goes beyond the surface-level understanding of a text and encourages students to challenge and question the assumptions that hide behind the story line. For example, many fairy tales promote the traditional gender roles of the strong, male hero and the beautiful female in distress who needs to be rescued. Critical literacy pushes students to examine these unstated gender roles and question the view of reality that is portrayed in such stories.

Using critical questions represents one way to facilitate a "skeptical stance" (Whitin & Whitin, 1998) in our students. Whitin and Whitin contend that skeptics know that "all [stories, texts] are covered with the fingerprints of storytellers who want to tell their own version of what happened" (p. 128). Helping students uncover those fingerprints allows them to challenge the unwritten assumptions that exist in many texts. Simpson (1996) offers seven different types of critical questions that can be used to facilitate discussion. Questions such as Whose voices aren't heard? Who is telling the story? and Whose point of view is presented and whose isn't? can be used to address the critical literacy notion that stories are selective versions of reality and that the version presented is dependent on who is telling the story and whose point of view is omitted.

Simpson (1996) describes an instructional process for implementing critical questioning in the classroom that is similar to the QAR minilesson described previously in this chapter. The basic QAR process I described—modeling the types of questions using a class read-aloud text, allowing students to generate their own questions, and having students practice discussing such questions in small groups—also can be used as the framework for a critical questioning minilesson. You may need to model a discussion of these types of questions, so rather than going straight into a student small-group discussion, lead the students in some whole-class discussions to help guide their efforts to challenge the hidden assumptions and representations of reality found in texts. If you would like more detailed information about what this type of lesson might look like, I encourage you to read Simpson's article listed in Box 3.3.

Box 3.3
Sources for Teaching Critical Questioning and Reading

Allen, A. (1997). Creating spaces for discussions about social justice and equity in an elementary class-room. *Language Arts, 74*(4), 518–524.

Simpson, A. (1996). Critical questions: Whose questions? *The Reading Teacher, 50*, 118–127.

Temple, C. (1993). What if Beauty had been ugly? Reading against the grain of gender bias in children's books. *Language Arts, 70*(2), 89–93.

Whitin, D., & Whitin, P. (1998). Learning is born of doubting: Cultivating a skeptical stance. *Language Arts, 76*(2), 123–129.

Although Marcy and I did not emphasize critical questioning in our literacy instruction, I strongly believe in the importance of developing critical literacy abilities in students and I encourage you to think about how you might include critical questioning in your instruction. The dialogue that follows will give you an idea of what a critical literacy discussion might look like in your classroom. The example is based on a segment from *The Great Gilly Hopkins* discussion group. The group is discussing Gilly and her use of "bad" language. As you read the transcript, try to identify places where critical questioning could have been included to challenge societal stereotypes and assumptions.

Michael: It was weird to hear a girl say that.

Jessie: Yeah, but that's the way she talks. It's the way she is.

Michael: I just thought it was weird because she didn't look like she would use that kind of language from the picture on the cover.

Jessie: Well, she does have messy hair in the picture. I thought it was weird that she would have on a girl shirt (the shirt has flowers on it) because she doesn't act like a girl. She acts more like a boy than a girl. Maybe she had to wear that shirt when they took her over to the Trotter's for the first time.

Michael and Jessie raise several issues that could have been elaborated on using critical literacy ideas. For example, Michael's comment that it was weird to hear a girl use bad language, and Jessie's comment that she had messy hair, could have been used to discuss assumptions such as, Is it more acceptable for males to use offensive language than females? What do people look like who are more likely to be thought of as someone who uses offensive language? Moreover, Jessie's comment that Gilly acted more like a boy than a girl could have been used to examine assumptions such as, What is acceptable behavior for boys and girls? Who decides what is acceptable? What happens when these unwritten rules of behavior are violated? Providing our students with instruction that addresses these types of critical literacy ideas allows them the opportunity to challenge and examine the stereotypic assumptions that exist in our society.

Reflection Point 3.5

1. Listen to your tape recorded discussions again. Are students asking critical questions?

2. Were there points in the discussion where a critical question might have been asked? What assumptions could have been challenged by asking such a question? How might you integrate this type of questioning into your literacy instruction?

Helping students to engage in grand conversations is not an easy or simple process—it is one that requires much hard work, persistence, and scaffolding. In this chapter, I have discussed three of the many possible scaffolding forms that can be applied in a classroom. As the examples in this chapter illustrate, students can sometimes use these scaffolding methods as crutches that inhibit a teacher's efforts to create grand conversations. But such methods also have the power to open up new avenues of understanding for students, as well as allowing them to bring their personal realities into their discussions. The only way we can determine whether our scaffolding methods are facilitating or constraining our efforts is to listen carefully to what our students are saying. When we keep them in sight, they provide a window that reveals the effect our scaffolding methods have on students' abilities to engage in grand conversations.

I would also like to underscore the need for us as teachers to continually examine our sometimes-hidden assumptions about what constitutes a thoughtful or "grand" conversation, and ask ourselves whether our assumptions are consistent with the realities of our students' lives. By asking these questions, we engage in a form of critical reflection similar to the critical literacy questions we encourage our students to ask. Just as we help them to uncover the hidden assumptions found in texts, we may discover that our own assumptions have the power to limit the possibilities we create. When I began to reexamine my assumptions about what constituted a thoughtful question or a grand conversation, I discovered a new level of respect and understanding for the realities and experiences my students brought to their discussions, and the exciting meanings they collectively created.

Integrating Skills Instruction With Literature Discussions

It's early October and we've just started the first cycle of literature discussions. Following today's discussions, Marcy led a whole-class debriefing to discuss how things went in the groups. After the debriefing, Marcy and I both had to laugh when Joseph asked, with a definite grimace on his face, "Do we have to do reading now?" Marcy laughed and said, "We just did! Do you mean the old way?" and Joseph responded, "Yes." How interesting that he did not perceive the whole literature discussion to be "reading."

Before she began working with literature discussion groups, Marcy used the district basal series and corresponding workbooks in her classroom, which is what Joseph was referring to as the "old way" in the above observation notes. Even when we started to implement literature discussion groups, they met only on Tuesdays and Thursdays; on Mondays, Wednesdays, and Fridays, Marcy still relied on the basal and workbooks for reading instruction. She was bothered by the discrepancy between the two approaches, and also by her students' continual complaints about having to do the workbooks. Although Marcy and her students preferred literature discussions, she was worried about covering the skills mandated by her district's curriculum and did not know how to integrate the two in a way that reflected her theoretical and philosophical beliefs regarding reading instruction. Joseph's comment illustrates that students are aware of the discrepancy in approaches as well, and they have strong feelings about each of them (also see student comments in Chapter 2, page 22).

I believe that Marcy's dilemma in trying to integrate these seemingly disparate aspects of reading instruction is a common one. Much has been written about the need for a "balanced" reading program; however, examples of how to actually achieve such a balance are harder to find. Often our tendency to categorize things into either/or dichotomies influences how we plan for and implement our instruction. This was the case for Marcy initially, as she felt that her instruction had to be either skills-based or literature-based. Such dichotomous thinking also is common in the research on literacy instruction—think about the ongoing debate between phonics and whole language—and this only serves to confuse teachers as to how we can achieve a balanced reading instruction program. The goal of this chapter is to present examples of how Marcy and I taught skills that are commonly found in district curriculum guides (e.g., vocabulary, story structure, theme, character development) within the framework of a literature study program utilizing literature discussion groups. It is important to point out that we did not simply follow the basal or workbooks in deciding what skills to teach. Rather, we looked at the district curriculum to see what skills were expected of students and then watched and listened for clues students gave us as to when they needed those skills taught. In planning the skills lessons this way, we assured ourselves that we were keeping Marcy's students' needs foremost in our sights rather than letting district curriculum guides or basal series dictate our instructional decision making. (For more information on a balanced approach to reading instruction, refer to the resources in Box 4.1.)

Reflection Point 4.1

1. Think back to your beliefs about reading instruction that you reflected on earlier in Chapter 1. Is your current skills instruction consistent with your beliefs about effective literacy instruction? Have you faced the same dilemma of having two seemingly disparate aspects to your literacy instruction (i.e., skills and literature discussions)? If so, how have you addressed this dilemma

in your own teaching? As you read this chapter, jot down ideas that appeal to you as ways to begin thinking about how you might integrate skills instruction into the literature-based aspect of your literacy program.

2. Considering Joseph's comment at the beginning of this chapter, how do your students respond to your skills instruction? How does their response to this type of instruction compare to how they respond to literature-based activities?

Box 4.1
Resources for Designing a Balanced Reading Program

Blair-Larsen, S.M., & Williams, K.A. (Eds.). (1999). *The balanced reading program: Helping all students achieve success.* Newark, DE: International Reading Association.

Braunger, J., & Lewis, J.P., (1997). *Building a knowledge base in reading.* Newark, DE: International Reading Association; Portland, OR: Northwest Regional Educational Laboratory; Urbana, IL: National Council of Teachers of English.

Braunger, J., & Lewis, J.P., (1999). *Using the knowledge base in reading: Teachers at work.* Urbana, IL. Newark, DE: International Reading Association; Portland, OR: Northwest Regional Educational Laboratory.

Fitzgerald, J. (1999). What is this thing called "balance"? *The Reading Teacher, 53,* 100–107.

Spiegel, D.L. (1998). Silver bullets, babies, and bath water: Literature response groups in a balanced literacy program. *The Reading Teacher, 52,* 114–125.

Weaver, C. (Ed.). (1998). *Reconsidering a balanced approach to reading.* Urbana, IL: National Council of Teachers of English.

Story Structure and Character Perspectives

I talked with Ethan and Scott today after their discussion of *The Face on the Milk Carton.* They talked at length about how they were confused by the book because it goes back and forth in time. They said, "In one point she'll be 5 years old and then on the next page she'll be 15 and driving." They found that very confusing and yet that never was a topic in their group discussion. (excerpt from my observation journal)

The *Julie of the Wolves* group was completely without discussion today. They said they were confused by the book but did not ask each other any questions to help clarify their confusion. They didn't know why she had run away or how young she was and so had no idea why her being married should be unusual. (excerpt from my observation journal)

After observing the above two groups, Marcy and I wondered if some students were having difficulty with the structure of their stories and would benefit from a strategy lesson on story structure. As Ethan and Scott noted, the structures used in many young adult novels (in their case a flashback structure) are more complex and difficult to follow than the basic story structure taught in the lower elementary grades. The basic story structure often focuses on story maps containing the elements of setting, characters, problem, events, and solution (Fitzgerald & Spiegel, 1983). These elements are usually found in a straightforward sequence in lower level books, which helps students learn the basic structure of narrative stories. However, this type of structure does not address more complicated structures, such as flashbacks, nor does it deal with internal motivations and reactions to events by characters.

A strategy that I have used to address these concerns is the Story Maps with Character Perspectives (SMCP) strategy (Emery, 1996). In the SMCP strategy, students first listen to or read a story and then list the important events, including the problem and resolution. Next, students discuss the perspectives of two characters during the main story events they have listed. This focuses students on the literary elements of both plot and character. In the section that follows, I describe how Marcy and I used this strategy with her students. For a more detailed description of how you might implement the SMCP strategy, see Emery's article in *The Reading Teacher* (listed in Box 4.2 on p. 77).

We began the lesson by using our read-aloud book, *Words by Heart* (Sebestyen, 1979), as a way to model the strategy. We had students brainstorm the important events that had happened in the book so far, and Marcy and I listed them on the board. As students offered suggestions, we asked the class where in the list each event should go and if they all agreed that it was an important event in the story. After we completed the list of events, we asked students to select two important characters from the book, and we used each character's name as the heading for a list on either side of the list of events. We then asked students to describe each character's perspective of, or response to, each of the events listed on the board. If the character had not been involved in the actual event, we asked students to hypothesize how they thought the character would have responded, or what the character's perspective would have been based on what they knew about the character.

After modeling the strategy, we asked students to listen to a short story that we used for guided practice. For this, we used the short story suggested in Emery's description of the strategy, "A Bad Road for Cats" (Rylant, 1985). We read the story aloud to the students and then asked them to complete the strategy sheet with their seating groups (see Appendix B for a copy of a sample strategy sheet). After the groups were finished, we discussed their lists of events and character perspectives as a whole class.

Following the guided practice, we gave students a blank SMCP sheet to complete with their literature discussion group as a way to practice using the strategy independently. Following are two examples from Michael and Hannah, who were reading *The Great Gilly Hopkins* and *Shiloh*, respectively (See Figures 1 and 2). As can be seen from these examples, the students were able to list the important events from their books and think about how the characters responded to the events. Marcy and I were particularly pleased to see many groups branch out from the usual "mad, glad, sad" type of character responses that students often give. Although Hannah still commonly used *glad*, *sad*, and *mad*, she also included reactions such as *excited*, *worried*, and *furious*. Michael's group showed a growing awareness of character reactions through their use of emotional descriptions such as *nervous*, *uncomfortable*, *anxious*, *hopeful*, *interested*, *determined*, and *surprised*. These types of responses showed Marcy and I that our students were beginning to explore more complex emotions in order to understand characters' reactions and motivations.

I found it interesting that after we did the SMCP strategy lesson, I never again sat in with or observed a group that claimed they were having trouble following a story. The one exception was the group reading *Cousins* (Hamilton, 1990). The girls in this group often talked about how the sequence of events on the day that one of the main characters dies was confusing. Kaitlyn used the idea of listing important events in her response log to help her keep the sequence straight. She wrote:

Notes

Major Time Parts

Figure 1
Michael's Story Maps With Character Perspectives (SMCP) Sheet

Book Being Read The Great Gilly Hopkins

Group Members Stan, Michael + Daria

Main character's perspective - how she/he feels	Important events in the story	Second character's perspective - how she/he feels
Gilly unhappy	/Gilly meets trotter/	trotter anxious
nervous, uncomfortable	/Gilly meets Mr R/	he thinks shes good.
feels smarter proud, mad	/Gilly meets Agnes/	proud, anxious
	/Gilly steals money/	
hopeful, anxious, nervous, intrested, suprised	/Tries to find her mom/	
	/Meets her grandmother/	glad determ- ined
sad, glad suprised	/Is told she will be living/	

1. Day camp

2. Lunch

3. Dolls

4. Trail Walking

5. Elodie's Shoe in the Lake

6. Pattie Ann's Death

Figure 2
Hannah's Story Maps With Character Perspectives (SMCP) Sheet

Book Being Read ___Shiloh_____

Group Members ___Hannah, Kaitlyn, Keely_____

Mardy		*Judd*
Main character's perspective – how she/he feels	Important events in the story	Second character's perspective – how she/he feels
happy, glad,		mad, upset
	mardy finds shiloh	
sad, upset, mad		happy
	he brings him to Judds house	
angry, stupid		angry
	Judd beats the dog	
happy, excited		mad, angry
	dog goes to mardys house again	
worried, happy to keep him	mardy builds cage	fearceouse
upset, angry, fedup		dont care
	german sheppard attacks Shiloh	
sad		dont care, mad at Shiloh.
	took him to the doctors.	

Kaitlyn used her list to help her group discuss what happened in the story on that day. Her list suggests that students were able to use the SMCP strategy to understand the more complex plot sequences found in some of their literature books.

Also after the SMCP lesson, I noticed that more students began to attend to characters' perspectives in their response logs and in their discussion. In her response log for the book *The Great Gilly Hopkins*, Keely wrote the following:

I think Gilly is a snot. But if I would have went to 9 foster homes I wouldn't be happy either.

In this entry, Keely evaluates Gilly's character but also tries to understand *why* Gilly might be the way she is. In trying to see things from Gilly's perspective, Keely is able to better understand the motivation behind much of Gilly's annoying behavior.

Students also revealed this attention to the character's perspective in their discussions. In the following transcript of the *Cousins* group, notice how the students tried to take into account three different characters' perspectives (Cammy's, Patty Ann's, and Patty Ann's mother's) as they discussed Patty Ann's death. This character's accidental drowning at a summer camp was witnessed by Cammy, and Patty Ann's mother initially blamed Cammy for her daughter's death.

Daria: And Patty Ann, she shouldn't have, you know, I understand that they're cousins and cousins fight, but in the beginning of the book when they got into that big fight, she still didn't have to say, "Well that's why Grandma Tutt's going to die." You know like that.

Regan: Yeah, that was rude. I think Cammy should just tell like she saw her go down and stuff instead of trying to hold it in that whole time. Towards the end she finally told.

Daria: Yeah but if you think about all the mean things that she has done to you, but still she would have said to you that's why Grandma Tutt's gonna die, but still, that's a sad thing to think about.

Tracey: I don't think Patty Ann was really all that bad, I mean, not *so* snotty that she was you know, really, really mean. I mean, she was a little bit mean, but not that bad.

Regan: You know, when they said that (reading from the book's back cover), "One day something really terrible happens, something that can't be changed," that's the day that Cammy learns the truth about Patty Ann, I think that's when they told her that she died, that was the part that something can't be changed, when Patty Ann was gonna die.

Daria: I feel sad to think about it 'cause there are cousins who fight but then you think they would make up or something. You predict that they would make up or something.

Kristine:	I think definitely that if Cammy found out that Patty Ann was gonna die, she would definitely make up, probably because that's really sad to think about, that someone's gonna die.
Regan:	When Patty Ann died, it changed Cammy's feelings about her you know (others nodding in agreement), the way she felt about her.
Daria:	And I guess she was like shocked because, um what's her name jumped to try to get her shoe and then Patty jumped and then she was maybe shocked and she didn't know what to do.
Regan:	I think Cammy wishes that she could bring Patty Ann back and make her troubles go all away.
Daria:	It's a scary thing to think about 'cause you know...
Tracey:	You can die any second.
Regan:	But Patty Ann was out of line when she said all that stuff about Gran Tutt.
Daria:	Yeah, look at her (looking at cover illustration), she looks like Miss Perfect. She thinks she's Miss Perfect and now she's not anymore.
Regan:	She could have at least tried to—
Daria:	—be friends with her.
Regan:	—appreciate her.
Tracey:	Would you want really long hair like that, down to your butt? I had hair, like, down here to my waist.
Regan:	I think Patty Ann, the number one reason she thinks she's Miss Perfect is that she has a pretty face and long hair.
Tracey:	But you know, I didn't think Aunt Effie had to be that mean to her because she's like, "Don't bother her either!" I mean, would your aunt be that mean to you?
Regan:	Cammy just came in there and watched her.
Daria:	Patty Ann's mom, you know, now she's blaming her for the death of her own daughter but they're cousins and that's her niece and I don't think that's right that she should blame her.
Regan:	My aunt would never be that mean.
Daria:	But you know, what if, OK, Patty Ann's mom is Grandma Tutt's daughter and Cammy is very close to Grandma Tutt.

> What if Grandma Tutt would talk some sense into Patty Ann's mom and say, "Well, it wasn't Cammy's fault that Patty Ann died, you know, she shouldn't have jumped in after a shoe, you know a shoe, it would have been long gone?"

Regan: I don't think Aunt Effie would listen. You know, Cammy didn't do nothing, she was just standing there in the doorway watching Patty Ann play the piano. She didn't do anything until Patty Ann had to say something when she finished.

Daria: You know, my aunt wouldn't be that mean to me.

Regan: Patty Ann's nothing but a snob but that's what Cammy was thinking you know in the beginning, but in the end she was crying inside, she couldn't get over it.

Daria: You know, you think about it too, after someone close to you dies, close to you in your heart, but you don't think about it as much as when they're alive, you're just mad at each other constantly, but in your heart, you know that—

Tracey: —you love 'em.

The students' discussion reveals how they began to discuss the perspective of multiple characters rather than only the main character, which is what we often saw in groups previous to the SMCP lesson. Here the students explored three different character perspectives. They felt Patty Ann was a snob who said rude things about Grandma Tutt and who thought she was better than Cammy because she was pretty and had long hair. Cammy was the helpless bystander who they felt was wrongly blamed by Patty Ann's mom (Aunt Effie) for Patty Ann's death. They identified with Cammy's feelings of guilt and sorrow over losing her cousin, but they also felt that Aunt Effie was mean to Cammy, and they struggled to understand how an aunt could be so hurtful to her own niece.

Before the SMCP lesson, we often heard groups discuss what they would do in a certain character's place, and students often related the character's experiences to their own. What was missing in these discussions, however, was an exploration of the character's motivations and perspectives. In the group's discussion following the SMCP lesson, the students worked to understand the perspective and motivations of the characters themselves. They still often placed themselves in the story and related to the events on a personal level, but their discussion broadened to include an examination of the characters and why they might have behaved or felt as they did.

In an effort to further expand students' understanding of character perspective, Marcy conducted a minilesson on how a book is influenced by who is telling the story. She read aloud *The True Story of the Three Little Pigs* (Scieszka, 1989), a rendition of the story of *The Three Little Pigs* as told from the wolf's perspective. After reading the book aloud, Marcy led a class discussion about how the book was different from the traditional *Three Little Pigs* story due to its alternative point of view. Although Marcy and I did not label it as such, this lesson was a form of the critical reading and questioning discussed in Chapter 3. By encouraging students to consider character perspective and point of view, we helped students to see how storytellers mark their stories with a particular version of reality. We saw the impact of this lesson on the *Cousins* discussion group:

Kristine:	Who was telling the story?
Regan and Daria:	Cammy.
Daria:	I wonder what it'd be like if we heard it from *her* point of view (pointing to Patty Ann on the book cover)?
Regan:	It'd probably be all different.
Kristine:	Yeah, but how can she tell it? She died. Like when it came to when she died, how would she say it?
Regan:	She could probably change the whole story around in her own words and make it seem like Cammy is a bad person (general agreement).
Tracey:	It really depends on who's telling the story. Like that one *Three Little Pigs* book that we read (all agree).

The students' discussion shows Marcy's minilesson was an effective way to focus students' attention on examining character perspectives and clarifying story structure issues. This type of lesson also provided Marcy with a way to address district-mandated skill instruction in an integrated format with her literature-based program, which was consistent with her beliefs about reading instruction. For more resources on how you might address the skills of story structure and character perspective or development in ways that are compatible with social constructivist theories and literature-based instruction, refer to the sources found in Box 4.2.

Box 4.2
Resources for Teaching Story Structure
and Character Perspective / Development

Emery, D. (1996). Helping readers comprehend stories from the characters' perspectives. *The Reading Teacher, 49,* 534–541.

Emery, D., & Mihalevich. C. (1992). Directed discussion of character perspectives. *Reading Research and Instruction, 31,* 51–59.

Fitzgerald, J., & Spiegel, D.L. (1983). Enhancing children's reading comprehension through instruction in narrative structure. *Journal of Reading Behavior, 15,* 1–18.

Idol, L. (1987). Group story mapping: A comprehension strategy for both skilled and unskilled readers. *Journal of Learning Disabilities, 20*(4), 196–205.

McConaughy, S.H. (1980). Using story structure in the classroom. *Language Arts, 57,* 157–165.

Shanahan, T., & Shanahan, S. (1997). Character perspective charting: Helping children to develop a more complete conception of story. *The Reading Teacher, 50,* 668–677.

Staal, L. (2000). The story face: An adaptation of story mapping that incorporates visualization and discovery learning to enhance reading and writing. *The Reading Teacher, 54,* 26–31.

Reflection Point 4.2

1. As you listen to your students' discussions this week, try to pay particular attention to how they discuss the plot line and characters in their books. Do students reading a book with a more complex story structure have questions about the sequence of events? Do they explore the characters' motivations, goals, and intentions? Do they discuss multiple characters' perspectives or focus predominately on the main character?

2. Try implementing a SMCP lesson with your students. What information does the lesson yield regarding your students' knowledge of story structure and character perspective?

3. Wait a week and listen to your students' discussions again. Do you hear any ideas from the SMCP lesson in their discussions?

Vocabulary Instruction

> Marcy and I met today to discuss the next cycle of literature books and also how I will begin to teach skills lessons during literature study time. Marcy and I looked through the curriculum guide to see what skills were emphasized and vocabulary seemed to be a big one. I looked at the basal workbook pages that addressed vocabulary and they were what I expected—fill-in-the-blank sentences using vocabulary words from the assigned story. I talked with Marcy about how that was a limited way to deal with vocabulary because it really depended on memorizing the words as the only strategy students could use. When students finally came across the words in the story, if they remembered what it meant from the workbook page, fine, but if not, they were stuck. So, we talked about how we might use context clues as an alternative strategy for teaching vocabulary words and decided to teach a context clues strategy lesson. (from field notes of discussion between Karen and Marcy)

We began our context clues lesson by having students brainstorm all the strategies they used to figure out the meaning of an unknown word in a story. Michael offered the strategy of using the words in the sentence or paragraph around the unknown word to help figure out what it meant. We used this comment as a springboard to introduce the concept of context clues and the purpose of the lesson.

To model the process of using context to determine the meaning of unknown words, Marcy used several sentences from the workbook. The sentences were relatively simple because they were written specifically to illustrate a certain type of context clue rather than as part of an actual text. For example, two of the sentences were,

> Instead of his usual happy manner, today Jeff seems quite *dejected*.

> The teacups were delicate, easily broken. So *fragile* that Ellen hardly dared to touch them.

In real texts, the author often does not provide the actual definition or literal examples of a particular word. Authors may provide clues, but the reader has to draw more from the surrounding context and his or her prior knowledge to determine the meaning of the word. However, these workbook sentences did provide an easy way to introduce the concept of context clues and to model different types of context clues such as synonyms (e.g., *delicate, easily broken*) and antonyms (e.g., *happy* and *dejected*).

For guided practice, we used examples from the read-aloud book *Words By Heart* (Sebestyen, 1979). These examples, drawn from a real text, were more challenging for the students and provided a way to further model how to use context clues and prior knowledge to figure out unknown words.

> Papa's way of thinking *perplexed* her. And what Claudie had said didn't make sense either. (p. 29)

Rather than placing the definition in the same sentence as the unknown word, as in many of the workbook examples, this excerpt illustrated that authors often will provide clues in the sentence preceding or following the sentence where the unknown word is found. Here, students used the phrase, "didn't make sense either," to help them figure out the meaning of the word *perplexed*. Noelia offered that *perplexed* probably meant something like *confused* and we agreed that *confused* would be a good synonym for *perplexed*.

> [Lena] took a long, sad breath. Then she grabbed the biggest book she could feel under the wagon sheet, plunged silently down the stairs, and slid it into her *satchel*. She went in and set the table for Mrs. Chism, numbed by her own *audacity*. (p. 37)

As students discussed the meaning of the word *satchel*, they used the clue that it is something in which you would put a book. Students offered substitute words such as *bag, purse, book bag*, and *backpack*. We then talked about whether people still use the word *satchel*. The students all said that they had never heard the word before, and that today Lena would probably call her satchel a book bag or backpack. This provided a perfect opportunity to discuss how the setting and time period of the story can affect the vocabulary that authors use.

Determining the meaning of *audacity* was more complicated for the students because the author did not provide explicit clues to help explain the word's meaning. This is more representative of the situation students are likely to encounter with unknown words, so it presented a good opportunity to guide students through the process of inferential reasoning. In this segment of the text, Lena took a huge risk in "borrowing" a book from her white, wealthy employer, Mrs. Chism, without asking her permission. We discussed how Lena must have been feeling as she debated whether to borrow the book or not. This brought up the idea that it was very risky and dangerous for Lena to do this and the fact that Mrs. Chism would definitely punish Lena if she found out. We then showed students how to use this information as they hypothesized what *audacity* might mean. Some suggestions offered by students were: "willing to take a risk," "having a lot of guts," "acting somewhat foolishly because she really wanted something." Although none of these suggestions will be found in a dictionary as a definition for *audacity*, Marcy and I were satisfied that students grasped the underlying concept. They learned how readers sometimes have to look beyond the words in the text and use their prior knowledge to help them figure out the meaning of unknown words.

Marcy continued to use the read-aloud book as a way to model and reinforce the idea of context clues for students. A few weeks later, she stopped after read-aloud time and said, "If I were discussing this chapter with my discussion group, I would have several vocabulary words to ask about." She then listed them on the board: *char, mattock, spade, maul, auger*. Marcy gave students the sentence in which each word occurred and directed each seating group to determine the meaning of a different one. Each group was successful in coming up with an acceptable definition for their word.

Marcy and I continued to watch and listen to students to determine if they were using the context clues strategy, but our efforts were in vain. We never heard even one group carry on a sustained conversation about an unknown word, nor did students write any unknown words in their response logs. When we reviewed the students' response logs at the end of the year, we found only one instance where a student wrote about a vocabulary term, asking "What is a terrible *ogre*?"

Initially, I was surprised by this because students in Clay and Roxanne's classroom frequently wrote unknown words in their response logs and brought them up in their discussions. Upon further reflection, though, I wonder whether this finding is so surprising after all. When I encounter a word I do not know while reading, I only stop to try to figure out its meaning if it is crucial to understanding the story. If my comprehension is not impeded by not knowing the exact meaning of the word, I am likely to continue reading. Consequently, I wonder if this is what Marcy's students did. Based on their discussions and response logs, it is clear that they comprehended their books, so it is perfectly reasonable to assume that they did not feel the need to stop and use the context clues strategy if their comprehension of the story was not affected by an occasional unknown word.

I am sure that Marcy's desire to address the skills mandated by her district is shared by many other teachers. I find it interesting, however, that in comparison with the positive effects of our SMCP lesson, which was motivated by an observed need in our students, our decision to teach the context clues strategy was based on emphasis in the district curriculum guide. Perhaps we should have listened to our students a bit more closely. They were not giving us any signs that they needed vocabulary help in their literature books, so it should not have been surprising that they did not suddenly start bringing up vocabulary words in their discussions.

This observation led me to ask further questions about how and why I teach context clues and other vocabulary strategies. Students are more likely to come across unknown words that are crucial to comprehension when they read expository, nonfiction, or content area texts. Therefore, it makes more sense to focus on vocabulary strategies with this type of text, rather than with the realistic fiction novels that our intermediate-grade students read for literature study. This is not to say that teaching vocabulary and context clue skills as a part of literature instruction is a waste of time. In fact, I think it may be easier for students to initially grasp the concept of context clues when reading their literature books because the conceptual load of these books is often less demanding than that of content area texts. Literature books often contain wonderful language that students should be encouraged to discover and explore. However, my observation of our students' complete disuse of this strategy during literature study time has made me wonder if perhaps students need more explicit instruction to attend to unknown vocabulary words when reading realistic fiction literature books, or if a more appropriate place to encourage students to practice using vocabulary strategies would be while reading content area texts. If you would like to read more about specific types of vocabulary strategies, including those that are typically used in conjunction with content area texts, refer to the resources found in Box 4.3.

Box 4.3
Resources for Vocabulary Instruction

Allen, J. (1999). *Words, words, words: Teaching vocabulary in grades 4–12.* York, ME: Stenhouse.

Blachowicz, C., & Lee, J. (1991). Vocabulary development in the whole literacy classroom. *The Reading Teacher, 45,* 188–195.

Fisher, P., Blachowicz, C., & Smith, J. (1991). Vocabulary learning in literature discussion groups. In J. Zutell & S. McCormick (Eds.), *Learner factors/teacher factors: Issues in literacy research and instruction. Fortieth yearbook of the National Reading Conference* (pp. 201–209). Chicago: National Reading Conference.

Manzo, A., & Manzo, U. (1997). *Content area literacy: Interactive teaching for active learning.* Upper Saddle River, NJ: Merrill/Prentice-Hall.

Rupley, W., Logan, J., & Nichols, W. (1998/1999). Vocabulary instruction in a balanced reading program. *The Reading Teacher, 52,* 336–346.

Reflection Point 4.3

1. As you listen to your students' discussions this week (or read their literature logs), listen for any discussion of unknown vocabulary words. Is this a part of their discussion?

2. Consider teaching a vocabulary strategy (the context clues lesson described previously, or a strategy from the resources in Box 4.3). How do students respond to the vocabulary lesson? Do they apply it to their literature books? How might you also incorporate vocabulary instruction into your students' reading of nonfiction texts?

Theme

Marcy and I decided to teach a strategy lesson on theme for two reasons. First, when we went through our observation sheets at the end of the first two literature study cycles, we noticed that none of the groups had discussed the theme of their book even though it was an item on the list of possible discussion questions. We interpreted this to be the students' way of telling us that determining the theme of a book was not a concept well understood by most of the class. Second, it was a required skill in the district curriculum, and we knew students would benefit from being able to apply this skill to their literature books.

My introduction to the theme lesson revealed our interpretation to be correct. I began by asking students to simply brainstorm what they thought the term *theme* meant. I was surprised that not a single student could give a plausible definition. Because I saw so many blank faces, I gave the students a generic definition to get us started. I wrote on the board that a theme is the message that the author is trying to get across to the reader. Tracey asked if that was similar to the moral of the story; I agreed, and several students nodded their heads in comprehension. I used our read-aloud book as a place to demonstrate what a theme might be in a book with which everyone was familiar. I started by saying that I thought one possible theme for our book, *Words by Heart* (Sebestyen, 1979), might be that people should not think they are better than others. I explained why I thought that might be a theme by listing events or character reactions from the book that related to that theme. After demonstrating this concept with our read-aloud book, I next used a book from a previous skills lesson, *Crow Boy* (Yashima, 1955), as a way to involve students in generating themes. I asked students what they thought the theme of *Crow Boy* was and they responded:

> **Noelia:** You shouldn't tease people who are different from you.
>
> **Tim:** Just because people are different doesn't mean they are stupid.
>
> **Hannah:** Everyone has talents.
>
> **Michael:** Don't judge a book by its cover.

We discussed each possible theme and students contributed events from the story to support them.

After the guided practice, I gave each seating group a different children's book to read. The students read the book as a group and discussed what they thought a possible theme might be for their particular story. I selected children's books because they could be read in a short amount of time, and I specifically chose children's books that had an identifiable theme. We used a different book for each seating group, but if you have multiple copies of a single book, you could have each group read the same book and then come back together for a class discussion of the various themes each group generated. See Box 4.4 for a list of possible children's books to use in a strategy lesson on theme.

Box 4.4
Children's Books to Use for a Strategy Lesson on Theme

Bunting, E. (1989). *The Wednesday surprise*. New York: Clarion Books.
Cannon, J. (1993). *Stellaluna*. New York: Harcourt Brace.
dePaola, T. (1979). *Oliver Button is a sissy*. New York: Harcourt Brace Jovanovich.
Hoffman, M. (1991). *Amazing Grace*. New York: Scholastic.
van Allsburg, C. (1993). *The sweetest fig*. Boston: Houghton Mifflin.

This strategy lesson spurred some discussion groups to begin talking about the theme of their books. This discussion from the *Cousins* group illustrates how the girls integrated their own personal experiences with text-based information to hypothesize about the theme of their book.

Tracey: What do you think the theme of the story is?

Regan: Try not to fight with your relatives.

Daria: Yeah, 'cause something terrible can happen.

Tracey: They can die any minute.

Daria: And you know, God says in the Bible if you fight, [and] I believe it's true, if you fight He will erase one day of your life that you're supposed to live.

Regan: And you just never know when you're gonna die.

Daria: Yeah, you just never know and it's a scary thing to think about. You can die tonight, you can die in school, you can die in your sleep.

Kristine: I know somebody who had gotten in a fight with his grandmother and then he said, it's a terrible thing to say, he said, "I hope you die of a heart attack" and this lady died the next week of a heart attack.

Regan: My old baby-sitter, Alonzo, died of a heart attack.

Tracey: Well, I know that if I die, I'm gonna go to heaven. So, it's a scary thing to think about, but, I mean, it's not that scary

	a thing to think about if you know you're gonna go to Heaven.
Regan:	How do you know you're going to Heaven?
Daria:	Yeah, 'cause there's some pretty nice people going to Hell these days.
Regan:	God doesn't need you, you know, he has all the power in the world.
Tracey:	Yeah, but, I mean—
Daria:	You gotta start living your life as a Christian. You can't just be going around and messing with people. It's a sad thing to think about.

When we went back through our observation notes, Marcy and I noticed that some students raised possible themes for their books in their discussions but these topics were not always picked up on by their group members. For example, in the *Face on the Milk Carton* group, Will said that there was no use fighting battles you can't win. While reading *Goodbye, Chicken Little* (Byars, 1985), Regan said that you shouldn't blame yourself when someone dies. Although these comments could have been developed into discussions of theme, Will's and Regan's groups chose not to do so and the topics were dropped. Students revealed their ability to identify theme in the strategy lesson and through class discussions of read-aloud books, but they did not choose to discuss the theme of their literature books on a regular basis. This observation has led me to wonder if students in the intermediate grades do not consider theme to be particularly relevant.

Marcy and I could have assigned thematic discussions, but we chose not to do so. We observed students having meaningful discussions about topics in their books that they found to be relevant to their own lives, and we both felt that had we assigned the topic of theme, we would have been imposing our teacher agenda on their discussions. In retrospect, though, I wonder if we should have stepped in more with this topic. Assigning students to talk about the theme of their books would not have precluded them from discussing other topics that they brought up on their own, and this would have been one way of assuring that students were getting sufficient practice at identifying theme. Moreover, it is possible that if we had made this a frequent assignment, students would have become more comfortable with the topic and it may have spontaneously found its way into their discussions.

Reflection Point 4.4

In a whole-class discussion, ask your students what "theme" means to them. Do their responses indicate a thorough understanding of the concept, or could they benefit from an explicit lesson on theme? Consider using a theme strategy lesson for your skill instruction this week. Are students able to apply the concept of theme to their literature books?

Learning how to integrate skills instruction into a literature-based program was an important goal for Marcy when we began our work together, and as Joseph's opening comment indicates, it was an important issue to address. In our final interview at the end of the year, Marcy reflected on this dilemma and her changing views regarding how skills and literature discussions might be integrated into a single, coherent literacy program.

> One of the big things I realized was that it doesn't have to be separate. Just because we're not maybe doing all of the pages in our workbook, that doesn't mean that we're not covering that, that I'm not teaching that, that they're not putting that into practice in some of their discussions. You know, even in the beginning of this year, discussion groups were on Tuesdays and Thursdays. Monday, Wednesday and Friday we went back to the regular old thing. [Now] it's been a long time since I've even looked in my reading manual. And even with the last unit in our workbook and skill pack, the kids were like, "Well, we didn't do all these pages, Mrs. Hyllberg." And I kinda looked over the pages but you know, we covered it all. And even when you were doing some of those lessons, that's when it really started making sense to me, that it doesn't have to be a separate thing. On [days we don't have discussion groups] I do focus still more on skills, but we tie them into the read-aloud book or to their literature books. Now when I teach a skill, their assignment or classwork will be to relate it to their specific literature group's story and I think that was more effective for them than doing a workbook page or story page. And it made more sense to them and they enjoyed it more, now that they had something to relate the skills to. Because otherwise it really doesn't make sense, if the skill is taught separately and it's not really being applied to anything. Whereas this way, they can apply it to their stories.

*Reflection Point 4.5*_____

Look back at what you wrote for Reflection Point 4.1 at the beginning of this chapter, along with the notes you have taken while reading. What new ideas have you read about that might help you address the questions and/or concerns you had regarding how to integrate the often disparate elements of skills instruction and literature discussions?

_____

Chapter 5

Assessing Literature Discussion Groups

> *Karen:* Why do you think we do the self- and peer evaluations in literature study?
>
> *Matt:* To see what we, you, what you will think that we want on our grade and then you don't like that grade then you'll just give 'em what you already had planned.
>
> *Karen:* What do you think I do with your evaluations that you do on yourself and your group members?
>
> *Matt:* Put 'em in the records or like keep 'em in one of the folders.
>
> *Karen:* Do you think I take into consideration the grade that you give yourself and your group members?
>
> *Matt:* Nuh-uh. You give us what you think you want us to get.

When I interviewed my class mid-year to hear their perceptions of how our literature study was going, it was with a heavy heart that I listened to Matt's perception of our assessment process. The process we used was one in which students completed a self- and peer assessment of their group members at the end of each cycle, which I then incorporated into my own assessments. I decided to use self- and peer assessments for several reasons. First, I wanted to use assessment techniques that would be consistent with my beliefs about the instructional practice of literature discussion groups, techniques that would allow for multiple voices, diminish my role as sole evaluator, and increase the students' voice in the assessment process. Specifically, I wanted my students to engage in the process of self-evaluation as a means to promote ownership of their learning and facilitate their efforts to become reflective, self-regulated learners. As Kathy Short and Gloria Kauffman (1992) point out, we often focus on the need to reflect on our students' learning as we evaluate and plan. We also must consider allowing our students to reflect on their own education, or we will keep them dependent on others to determine what is a valued indication of learning. The idea of helping individuals become self-regulated learners was important to me because the students were conducting their own discussions; I could not be present in every group. They needed the opportunity to develop the skills necessary to control their own learning process and to assess their processes and products. Thus, I wanted to incorporate an assessment tool in my classroom that would provide my students with a means to reflect on their own learning. I wanted them to be able to ask and answer the questions, What have I learned? and Is what I have learned valuable? However, as Matt's response clearly revealed, my reasons for using self- and peer assessments were not understood or shared by many of my students.

My second reason for using this type of assessment was that interpersonal relationships among my students were problematic, and the success of literature discussion groups often hinges on the students' ability to work together. I wanted an assessment tool that would take into account the social nature of this type of learning and the responsibility shared by all members in determining the learning that occurs in such a context. In the section that follows, I describe how I used self- and peer assessments in my classroom in Tuscon and my students' perceptions of this type of assessment process.

Reflection Point 5.1 _____

1. How do you assess your students' literature discussions? What are your reasons for using these assessment measures?

2. Look back in your journal to the beliefs about literacy learning and instruction that you wrote in Chapter 1. Are your assessment practices consistent with your beliefs?

3. What concerns or questions do you have regarding how to use literature discussion groups in your literacy assessment practices? As you read this chapter, keep this list close by and jot down notes when you see an idea that might help you address your questions or concerns.

Self- and Peer Assessments: A Look at My Classroom

At the end of each literature cycle, students filled out an evaluation sheet (see Appendix C) on which they evaluated both their own and their group members' performance for that cycle. The students gave a rating for each member and had to provide a rationale for each rating. The rating scale we used, which was decided on by my students, was as follows:

+ for Excellent,

√+ for Really Good,

√ for OK,

√- for Needs Improvement, and

- for Not Acceptable.

Before we did the first evaluation, the students brainstormed criteria that they could use to evaluate themselves and their group members. In the first cycle, they generated a rather short list of behaviors such as don't fool around, cooperate, talk about the book, and don't fight. Because I wanted the students to have ownership over this process, I allowed the list to end there instead of stepping in and adding my own more "teacherish" criteria. These criteria were then listed on the back of the evaluation form so that students could refer to them when completing their evaluations.

During the next literature cycle, we periodically revisited the criteria during our whole-class debriefing time to see if they needed any modifications. The students usually decided to include additional criteria that emerged from the debriefing sessions and from their increased experience in conducting literature discussions. For example, one session focused on a group that was having difficulty with students listening to each other. They decided that "listening when others talk" needed to be added to our list of criteria. On another day, I conducted a minilesson on the importance of stating your own opinion and supporting it by explaining why you felt or thought that way. In the debriefing session, students decided that "stating opinions and telling why" needed to be added to our criteria list. I could also add criteria to the list during these discussions, but I usually found that by conducting the focused skill lessons, students were able to make the connection between the lesson and evaluation and add the appropriate criteria on their own. When we discussed the criteria at the end of the second literature cycle, the students decided that they could be divided into two categories: Cooperates With Group and Participates in Group (see Table 1 for actual criteria in each category). It was this set of criteria that students used for the rest of the year.

Table 1
Criteria Used for Literature Group Discussion Assessments

Cooperates With Group	*Participates in Group*
sits in the circle	talks about the book
talks nicely	helps others in group
does not argue	gives opinions and says "why"
does not fool around	asks questions
listens	responds with reasonable answers
does not hurt others' feelings	gives detail
reads the book	
stays with the group	

After students completed their self- and peer assessments, I recorded the results in my gradebook and used their ratings to help me determine an overall literature study rating for each student in that cycle. This was a three-step process.

1. I went back over my observation notes (see pages 105–110 for a further explanation of these notes), and determined a rating for each student based on my perceptions of how well they had talked about their book and their overall behavior during discussions.

2. I averaged the ratings given to a student by his or her peers. For example, Deonte's group members gave him ratings of √, √+, √+, and √+. This worked out to an average rating of √+.

3. I took the student's self-assessment rating, their peer-assessment rating, and my rating and averaged the three to determine an overall rating for that literature study cycle. For example, Deonte gave himself a √ rating. Based on my observation notes, I had assessed his performance and literacy abilities at the same level. Therefore, his overall literature study rating was an average of √+ (peer assessment), √ (self-assessment), and √ (my assessment). This came out to an overall rating of √, which was the final rating I recorded in my gradebook for that literature cycle.

Assessment Is a Learned Process

When asking students to complete self-assessments, it is important to keep in mind that learning to evaluate is a process. As I read through my students' self- and peer assessments after the first literature cycle, I reminded myself that this was only the beginning. The students' first assessments were very general and the overwhelming focus of their evaluations was on whether the group members were working or playing around. Zenobia's evaluation was typical in its emphasis on how much work was done and vague reasoning (see Figure 3).

Other typical comments included: "I worked hard but goofed off once," "She was always playing around with her stuff she brought with her," and "I worked good and hardly ever goofed off." In this initial cycle it seemed that working or not working was sufficient reason to give someone either a high or low rating. There was virtually no concern with whether students were actually reading or discussing their books.

As we continued to discuss the criteria and students gained experience in conducting literature discussions, their evaluations reflected a growing understanding of how to apply the criteria in their evaluations. For example, consider Jeralyn's evaluation from our third literature cycle (see Figure 4).

In this evaluation, Jeralyn used explicit reasoning and broadened her focus to include multiple types of criteria—from both the Cooperates With

Figure 3
Zenobia's Peer Assessment From the First Literature Cycle

Chocolate Touch
Literature Group

Name Zenobia

Group Members	Grade	Reason - How did person work in group?
1. Yourself	+	because I asersed every quiestion and everthing
2. Stacey	+	because she did everthing
3. Curtis	✓−	he did nothing
4. Nicole	✓	she did half of everthing
5. Daniel	✓+	he did half of everthing
6. Chris P.	+	he did everthing
7. Amanda	+	she did everthing

rading Scale:

Excellent ✓+ Really Good ✓ O.K. ✓− Needs improvement

— Not acceptable

Figure 4
Jeralyn's Peer Evaluation From the Third Literature Cycle

Literature Group Evaluation   Name _Jeralyn_____

Book _Gilly Hopkins_____

Group Members	Rating	Reason
1. Yourself Me Jerily	√+	Becous I did good. I was a little Behind, But I sat in the Circle listend and talk niely about the Book.
2. Rayon	+	Becous he did to read ahade But he sete listend and responded. he helped others and asked questions.
3. Lajuano	+	Becous she talks about the Book with our fooling around, she also asks other people questions and gives detcl.
4. Richerd	√+	Becous he diden't ague of hart fellings, in he talks about Book and gives responsuble ansers.
5. Mikel	√+	Becous he did good and almost alaws cape up with the group.
6.		

Scale: **+** Excellent **√+** Really Good **√** O.K. **√—** Needs Improvement

— Not Acceptable

Group and Participates in Group sections—to evaluate herself and her group members. This was a distinct improvement from the general comments and narrow focus on work issues found in many of the first cycle evaluations. In particular, I was relieved to see the growing emphasis on participation and book-related responses. Students were giving reasons for their evaluations, such as:"He helped others,""She asked good questions,""She gave a lot of detail," and"He always gave his opinion and said why."

Students also began commenting on whether their group members were keeping up with the reading or reading ahead. In the third cycle, I found numerous comments addressing these issues:

- "She read to the parts we were supposed to and did not read further than us."

- "I got caught up with my group in the chapters and did not skip any chapters."

- "I wasn't perfect and also got ahead of my group but the good part is that I tried my best to discuss where the rest of my group was at."

The increased emphasis on the need to stay on track with the reading provided a perfect opportunity for me to address this issue in our whole-class debriefing sessions. We discussed how not reading or reading ahead affected the group's discussion and brainstormed suggestions for how to deal with this issue. For example, Dag said that if you read ahead you need to be sure you do not"give away"information in the discussion that the rest of your group has not yet read. Jackie suggested that if there were people who never read to where they were supposed to, you could offer to partner read with them during SSR to help them keep up. I was particularly pleased with Jackie's response because it revealed that students were beginning to understand the social aspect of this type of learning environment, and were willing to assume responsibility for helping each other succeed.

The students' broadening focus to include more book-related criteria did not eliminate the work criteria. However, I noticed that in later cycles students addressed work issues within a framework that also included participation and reading concerns. This broadened conception of work issues is illustrated by the comments of Kefira and Ryan, two strong-willed students who frequently clashed with each other as members of the group reading *The War With Grandpa* (Smith, 1984). This book was a challenge for Kefira, a struggling reader who qualified for support services, but it was read easily by Ryan. On their evaluations, Kefira wrote about herself, "I worked hard and read the book." Ryan's evaluation of Kefira supported her self-evaluation. He wrote, "She worked hard on getting through the book." These responses revealed that the students no longer viewed "work" as simply "not fooling around," but that the concept of work was connected to the actual reading of the book. Seeing this type of improvement helped to assure me that my students were growing in their ability to engage in the process of self-reflection, and were using this process to become self-regulated learners.

What Students Had to Say About Self- and Peer Assessment

Because engaging in self- and peer assessment was new for most of my students, I wanted to hear their perceptions of this process. Therefore, I interviewed all of my students in January, and again in May, to hear their thoughts and find out if their perceptions had changed over the course of the year. When I read through the two sets of interview transcripts, it became apparent that two main themes were most important to my students. The first theme was that of student voice and ownership in the assessment process. The second theme was related to issues of honesty and dishonesty in the evaluations. The students' perspectives regarding each theme are described more fully in the following section.

The Role of Student Voice in the Assessment Process

> Because it might help you [the teacher] a little? Because you look at 'em and then you like the people's opinions sometimes and sometimes you don't.
>
> Susie

> Because you [the teacher] can't really decide what you're gonna give us and you want to see what we want to give ourself. And [I might say] I'm

gonna give myself an A but you can't do that because it's your, the teacher's, decision what to give us.

Matt

I think it's because to let you [the teacher] know how the group did together and how much teamwork they have.

Alana

Because, um, if we do it that way with, um, on the paper and why we gave 'em the grade, you [the teacher] can find out if they've been acting up and if I've been reading the book.

Kefira

Probably to see how we grade and our responses and then you [the teacher] can find out by our responses to grade us yourself. It helps you because we're telling things that they did wrong or right and then you can probably decide off those.

Johnny

These responses, given to me in January by my students, were an eye-opener. I wanted my students to use self- and peer assessments as a way to develop more ownership of their learning, but it was clear that this was not happening. Although several students referred to giving their opinion as a reason for why we were doing assessment this way, it was apparent that they did not know why that was important. Moreover, there was a sense that they viewed the purpose of providing me with feedback on peers as a way to tell who was and was not working in the groups—functioning as a tattling mechanism rather than a process of self-reflection. Students felt that the predominant reason for doing assessment was to give me information that I could use in my grading. Even though they might give me their opinion, I, as the teacher, still held the real power. I had the final say in what their grade would be; I did the real grading.

Even more distressing to me was that several students did not believe I used the ratings that they gave me in my assessment. This was made painfully clear by Matt's comments and, unfortunately, he was not alone in his views. Comments made by Matt and other students revealed that many of them firmly believed they merely went through the motions of self-assessing. When it came right down to it, I still had the power to determine what grade a student received. Most troublesome to me, however, was my students' seeming acceptance of such a practice. It was as if they were so accustomed to having no voice in their learning that when given an opportunity to speak they still did not believe their voice would be listened to or valued. This realization led to an immediate mini-lesson on how I used the ratings from both their self- and peer assessments, along with my observations, to determine their literacy grade.

Thankfully, the students' perceptions changed by May of that year. During the end-of-the-year interviews, several students still talked about the evaluations as a way to provide me with information, but their reasons for why this was important had undergone a significant change. Rather than being a tattling mechanism, students now talked about the peer evaluations as being a more legitimate way to assess themselves and their peers. As Jackie stated,

> I thought it was good because like the teacher, you don't always know what the group did and stuff like that so I thought it was kind of interesting to let the students that knew what each other were doing to do the grading.

It also was obvious that students now believed I used their evaluations and that their voices were as important as mine. For example, Jamie said,

> I think that's better than you giving us a grade because then when you give us a grade we think it's not fair because we don't think we deserve that grade but when we write it down—what *we* think—and we give it to you, and you take it into consideration and maybe our grades will change.

There was no longer the sense that I held the real power and gave the real grades; students held an equal place in the assessment process. They now viewed the process as an opportunity to engage in self-reflection and as a means of having a legitimate and valued voice in their learning assessment. This newfound sense of ownership was perhaps most evident in Deonte's response. When asked how he felt about our literature study evaluations, he replied,

> **Deonte:** Yeah, because you know that, like, so if I got an F, I'd be the one who put it on my paper because if you [teacher] put it on, I'd get all upset and stuff because this ain't, I'd be saying like, "Oh I didn't get that, she's just doing that to make me feel bad."

> **Karen:** Do you think you learned anything from having to do your own evaluation?

Deonte: Yeah, because when you get an F, you think, well so my teacher just gave me that, and then when you give yourself an F, you go, yeah I did really bad on that stuff.

I was troubled by the fact that many students believed they were often graded unfairly by their teachers (as implied by Deonte's and Jamie's comments). Ryan shared this view in his interview:

> You know, lots of kids get mad when teachers grade kids. My friend, he got a very bad grade in math at my old school and he didn't like that. He got so mad he went out and got in a fight with lots of kids. [This way] gives us a chance to say what *we* thought of how we did.

These responses only served to reinforce my belief that our students need opportunities to engage in the process of self-assessment, and that such opportunities have the potential to help them take ownership of their learning and have a voice in determining what was learned.

Even as I advocate the need for self-assessment, I can hear the voice in many teachers' heads saying, "Yes, this all sounds great, but how do we know our students will be honest in their evaluations?" I had this same concern and so did my students. In the next section, student perceptions of honesty in assessment will be addressed. Hopefully, they will lay to rest some of your worries about this issue.

Honesty in Student Assessments

> I think we should just let you pick the grades because, like, if a person gets mad at another person, then they'll just give'em a bad grade anyway 'cause they're mad at'em.
>
> Lajuana

> Sometimes [people are honest] and sometimes they aren't because I know it's pretty hard because if like, you gave your friends a small grade but it was the truth, they'd get mad at you. Sometimes they would just give you a high grade.
>
> Maria

> I think that it's very good but I think some people, they might, 'cause they don't like this person, they might give'em a low grade.
>
> Zenobia

> I don't think we should do that because other people they've been having troubles with like, I heard one of my classmates say, "I'm gonna give 'em a bad grade just because I don't want 'em in my group."
>
> Kefira

These comments, made by my students in January, left little room for doubt that many of them were certain their peers were not being honest in their evaluations. But when I compared the students' peer evaluations to those of their other group members and to my own observations, I found that the majority of students were giving themselves and their peers appropriate ratings. However, as honesty was such a major theme in the students' responses, I emphasized the importance of being honest in my minilesson on how I used the peer evaluations in the determination of grades. I continued to reinforce the need for honesty during the whole-class debriefing sessions before students completed the evaluation forms.

In May, honesty was still an important issue, but the reason for its importance had shifted. By this time, the majority of students felt that their peers were being honest in their evaluations. Maria's earlier comment alluded to this when she stated that because people were being honest in their evaluations, students were receiving grades that were fair and accurate. Daniel echoed this belief, saying "I was happy about [the way I was graded] 'cause they'd probably have to be honest and then you would be honest so then we'd get the grade we really deserved." Instead of focusing on the honesty of their peers, students now saw honesty as an aspect of *self*-assessment and a necessary component of taking ownership for their learning. As Bart said,

> Because like whenever you grow up, that's what part of life is like, like the earth. It's how, it's like you could see something [on the ground] and just leave it there and not pick it up. That's like grading yourself on how good you do on like keeping the earth clean.

Listening to my students' changing perceptions about self- and peer assessment raised many issues for me as a teacher. I realized that before self-assessments can be used effectively as a means of self-reflection, students first need to believe in the legitimacy of the process. When my students did not believe their assessments served any real purpose and did not count toward their real grade, there was little motivation to take them seriously. I cannot help but wonder if part of the reason so many of my students viewed the assessment process as unfair in the beginning was due to their prior experiences with evaluation. Most of my students had not had a great deal of success in school and, as revealed by many of their responses, they often felt they had been evaluated unfairly by teachers making unilateral decisions in which they had no say. It was clear that my students initially felt teachers had sole power in determining grades; if students did not agree with the grades they received, they had no options other than to accept the grades given to them. It is possible that my students had come to believe that the grades given to them by teachers did not reflect how they perceived themselves as learners, and so they had come to mistrust any type of assessment. If they did not believe that their teachers were being fair or honest in determining their grades, what motivation did they have for being honest when engaging in self- and peer assessment?

I had to trust my students if I wanted to have a classroom where they and I shared power and where they could assume ownership of their learning. After I discovered my students' mistrust of teacher-driven assessment, it became even more imperative that I trust and validate my students' initial efforts to engage in self-reflection and assessment of their learning. But there was a larger issue at stake than merely seeing if my students were being honest. I knew that if they were to become reflective, self-regulated learners who assumed ownership for their learning, honesty had to be a component of that reflection. But they first had to believe that I was being honest with them, and that their assessments would be used to determine their grades. As I discovered, my students needed to see concrete proof of my process through explicit examples of how I used their assessments in my grading.

I had to keep in mind that learning to engage in self-reflection takes time. I could not expect my students' first attempts at self-reflection and self-assessment to be perfect representations of their actual performance and learning. Even the adult students in my graduate-level classes find it difficult to self-assess their work. My fifth graders were no different; but as they came to believe they were being given a legitimate voice in the assessment of their learning, their concerns over honesty shifted from a fear that others were not being honest to a recognition of the need to be honest with themselves. As a result, their later self-assessments were much more accurate representations of their learning.

Reflection Point 5.2

1. Select a few representative students from your class and ask them what they think about how they are assessed in literacy. Do their perceptions match your reasons for your assessment methods stated in Reflection Point 5.1?

2. What are your students' perceptions of grades? Do they feel they are something to be earned? given? used as punishment? Do they feel their grades accurately reflect their learning?

Assessment Versus Grading

Listening to my students' perceptions of our self-assessment process and their initial belief that their assessments did not really matter raised a dilemma for me in trying to separate assessment from grading. Although the two usually are discussed separately and often are perceived to serve different functions, my students' voices gave me pause to rethink the implications of keeping assessment and grading separate. As I stated earlier, I wanted students to have a voice in their assessment to promote reflection on, and ownership of, learning. But my students' January interview responses made it clear that without a direct connection between their self-assessments and grades, there was little valid reason for them to engage in the self-assessment process. I might consider processes such as self-regulated learning, student reflection, and self-assessment worthy in their own right, but my students did not. It was not until they came to believe that their self-assessments influenced their actual grades that they began to see the value in self-assessment and reflection.

As educators, we know the power that grades have, and to deny that power and expect our students to engage in self-assessment as a process completely separate from grading seems somewhat dishonest to me. As long as we are forced to put a single letter on students' report cards to represent their learning, we must acknowledge our students' need to know that their self-assessments will influence the evaluation that carries the most weight—their grades. Without that direct connection, it may be futile to expect students to appreciate the value in self-assessing merely for the sake of reflecting on their learning.

However, I still am not convinced that such a connection between self-reflection and grading is necessary or optimal. I do not want to equate assessment with grading. I want my students to have ways other than grades to define themselves as learners. Students' sense of mistrust and concomitant feeling of powerlessness to change how they are evaluated and viewed as learners underscores my belief that children need opportunities to engage in reflection. If teacher evaluations are the only means by which students determine how they see themselves as learners, they have no options other than to adopt the label of "unsuccessful learner" provided by these external sources. Reflecting on their learning through the process of self-assessment represents one method we can use to help our students form their own perceptions of themselves as learners. So even though I understand my students' need for a direct connection between self-assessment and grading, I still hold on to my belief that reflection and self-assessment are worthy processes in their own right, separate from single letter grades on report cards. As it stands now, the dilemma of assessment versus grading remains unresolved for me.

Reflection Point 5.3 _____

1. Take a few minutes to write down your thoughts on this dilemma. How do you feel about self-assessment, student reflection, and grades? What relationship, if any, do you see among these constructs?

2. Do you encourage your students to reflect on their learning? What is your purpose for having students self-assess or reflect on their learning, and how do you use their assessments/ reflections?

Teacher Assessment

The cornerstone of my literature discussion group assessment was observation. By observing my students and listening carefully to how they talked about their books, I was able to use what Yetta Goodman (1978) calls "kidwatching" to assess how my students were progressing and to plan for subsequent instruction. This planning aspect is important because as Regie Routman (1994) reminds us, unless we are using the observation data we collect to inform and guide our instruction, we are not really evaluating; we are merely amassing bits and pieces of information. As I describe my observation process, please keep in mind that observation is a skill that develops with time, patience, and practice. I needed generous amounts of practice before I felt comfortable using this type of assessment tool in my classroom.

One of the most difficult, but most important, parts of using observation effectively is knowing what we are *looking for* in our observations. Therefore, before I began to observe my students, I sat down and decided what literacy behaviors I wanted and expected to see students exhibit during literature discussions. I thought about my beliefs regarding literacy learning, as well as what I knew about fifth graders' literacy development and the types of skills they should possess at this age. The resulting list resembled the list found in Figure 5 (although this is a continuous process and the list is constantly being revised). Creating this initial list was a starting point for clarifying what I would be actively looking and listening for as I observed my students in their literature discussion groups.

Reflection Point 5.4

Before reading further, take time to generate a list of indicators of your students' literacy abilities. Your list will look different from

Figure 5
Literacy Indicators to Look for When Observing Literature Discussions

Uses prior knowledge to construct meaning
Relates book to personal experiences
Makes predictions
Uses the text to support predictions
Imagery
Personally identifies with character(s)
Evaluates characters
Places self in the story
Questions the author
Connects the book to other texts
Asks questions to further understanding
Draws inferences
Retells/Summarizes
Identifies theme
Uses context to determine unknown vocabulary

mine because yours will be influenced by your own beliefs, philosophy, background, and experiences, but you can use my list as an example to get you started. As you write, ask yourself, What is it that you value in literacy and literature discussions? What would you like to see and hear students discussing in their literature groups? What would you need to hear them talking about to know they are growing as readers?

After I made my list of literacy indicators it was time to put them into practice and begin my attempts to use observation as an assessment tool. To do this, I simply used a clipboard with sheets of lined paper to write observation notes as I sat in with various discussion groups. At this point, I only tried to write the content of what students said; I did not try to analyze or reflect on their statements. I did, however, keep my list of literacy indicators in the back of my mind. When a student said something that directly related to an indicator, a flag went up for me and I tried especially hard to get an accurate note of what he or she said. My observation notes for the *Cracker Jackson* group in Marcy's classroom (see Figure 6) are hastily scribbled paraphrases, rather than verbatim accounts of students' statements.

Figure 6
Observation Notes From *Cracker Jackson* Group

May 8
Cracker Jackson

Noelia – retell; my mom find out if took car; why C. not go straight to hospital – I would have; wonder if he beating her before married?; go back to him b/c she has so many times before

Jessie – retell; B.R. find way to get out of jail; N. might die; B.R.'s mom stupid b/c thinks it's OK to hit A.; B.R. promise not to hit

Kari – A. go to Avondale; won't put up w/ it anymore; mad at B.R.

Amy – – retell; baby hasn't opened eyes yet; who can believe B.R.?; maybe put make-up on bruises; I covered up black eye w/ make-up; A. should go to Avondale

Noelia – have uncle who gets drunk + really bad; TV shows bad b/c so violent; hard to think of someone you love getting hit; I'm very protective of my family

Jessie – even if B.R. promise, he'll get drunk + do it anyway; he should go get punching bag; B.R.'s mom needs help too; N. will learn hitting + just pass it on

Amy – B.R. should get help for alcohol problem; funny watch drunk people if not family members – gives example; mostly B.R.'s father's fault b/c he see father beat mom; if I were A., I'd pack up + leave

These types of observation notes would be described as "raw notes" by qualitative researchers because they were recorded in an effort to get the actual content of talk down rather than to interpret what was said. The reason for keeping note taking and interpreting separate is that interpretation takes time and mental energy. I found that if I tried to interpret what students said while simultaneously writing down what they were saying, I missed important parts of the conversation. Consequently, when you first try this technique I recommend only writing down the content of student discussions—save the interpretation for later.

Reflection Point 5.5

Observe a literature discussion group and take notes on what you hear. Try to keep your list of literacy indicators in mind as you listen and write. How do these indicators inform your observations? Do they help you pay attention to particular pieces of conversation more closely? Do they help you know what you are listening for?

I usually was able to sit in with two or three discussion groups every day. This allowed me to observe each group multiple times during the course of a literature cycle, which is important in order to get a representative picture of the students. Gathering multiple instances of observation data to use in our assessment of students lessens the likelihood that our observations will resemble the type of one-shot assessment tools we are trying to avoid (e.g., end of book tests, projects).

After I collected a few days' worth of observation notes, I began to interpret this data using my literacy indicators to create an observation grid (a blank copy of this grid can be found in Appendix D). By directly connecting my observation notes to these indicators, I could assure that my assessments would be based on my literacy beliefs and goals. I then read back over my observation notes and decided what literacy indicator was represented by each student's comments. For example, look at Noelia's comments in Figure 6. I interpreted the observation note, "Wonder if he beating her before married?" as fitting the literacy indicator of Asks Questions to Further Understanding, and so wrote Noelia's comment in the box on my grid for that indicator (see Figure 7 for a copy of Noelia's grid). I placed her comment, "Go back to BR because she has so many times before" in the Makes Predictions box, and interpreted her comment, "Uncle who gets drunk really bad" as an example of the indicator Relates to Personal Experience. I continued to do this for each observation note for each student. I also read through students' literature logs and transferred that information to the observation grid as well. By using both discussion observations and literature log entries, I was able to obtain a more complete picture of how the student was engaging with the text. This also helped assure that I was getting data for students who were less vocal in the actual discussions and preferred to respond to their book primarily through written response.

I want to note that engaging in this type of assessment can be time-consuming. However, I discovered that the process became much quicker after the first few literature discussion cycles. I encourage you to remember this, and not to get discouraged when you try it for the first time. With practice, I found that this type of assessment was not substantially more time-consuming than grading traditional worksheets and had the added advantage of providing me with a much more valid picture of my students' comprehension.

After I interpreted my raw notes and transferred the notes to the observation grid, Marcy and I were able to use this tool to determine the students' strengths (both individual and whole-class), and to decide on a direction for our subsequent instruction. To do this, we looked over our students' charts at the end of each literature cycle to see which indicators were not being displayed (as revealed by empty boxes). If we saw that a particular indicator box was blank for the majority of students, we knew that the students would benefit from some explicit instruction in this area. By using the observation grids in this manner, we assured that we were teaching the skills actually needed by our students. In other words, we were able to keep our students *in sight* as we planned for instruction.

I also used the observation grids for individual student assessment purposes. For example, I could determine a student's strengths by looking at his or her chart and seeing what types of indicators were exhibited on

Figure 7
Noelia's Observation Grid of Literacy Indicators

Noelia — Cracker Jackson

Uses prior knowledge to make meaning	Relates to personal experience	Makes predictions	Uses text to support predictions	Imagery
- explains what a leech is—sucks blood - T.V. shows bad because so violent	- get hit w/ football but not get black eye - my mom would find out if I took coin - uncle who gets drunk - had to think of someone you love getting hit; I'm very → protective of my family	- something happen to A. or C. but not the baby - A. will go back to B.R. because she has so many times before		
Personally identifies with a character	**Evaluates character** - C.'s dad never been serious, that's why they divorced	**Places self in the story** - would call police + call to see if A. is ok - I would have gone straight to the hospital	**Questions the author**	**Connects to other texts**
Asks questions to further understanding - Wonder why C. not go straight to hospital? - Wonder if B.R. beating A. before they got married?	**Draws inferences** - thinks C. knows but not tell because might be scared that B.R. find out, A. get beat even more - B.R. not like C. because C. knows	**Elaborates on others' comments** - yes - explains Jessie's question - explains Amy's question	**Retells / Summarizes**	**Identifies theme** - protecting family
Vocabulary / Uses context	**Materials:** Book – yes, yes Read – yes, yes Response Log – yes, yes		**Miscellaneous**	

a regular basis (evidenced by lots of comments written in those boxes). I also could determine areas that needed further development by looking across the student's charts from different literature cycles to determine what literacy indicators were not being revealed (as evidenced by blank boxes in charts for several books). It was important for me to look at a student's chart for more than one book before making this type of decision, because there was always the possibility that a student said something in a discussion that I was not around to hear. If the box for an indicator was blank for two or more books, however, I felt more comfortable interpreting that to mean that the student had not fully developed a particular skill.

Reflection Point 5.6

Using the list of literacy indicators you generated earlier, create an observation grid. Go back to the observation notes you took and interpret them in relation to your literacy indicators, transferring your notes to the grid. What patterns do you see? Are there literacy indicators that students use consistently in their discussions? Are there others that are not found in students' discussions?

You may need to collect more observation data before such patterns become apparent. If so, try collecting observation notes again and interpret those notes to see what your students are revealing to you about their strengths and areas that need more development.

But I Still Have to Give a Grade on the Report Card

Observation assessment may sound good in theory, but we still have to give a single letter grade on students' report cards. How do we reconcile these two seemingly opposite types of assessment? I faced this dilemma, and I will describe the process Marcy and I used to incorporate our observation data from literature study groups with the district's report card.

The report card for Marcy's district had an overall category titled Reading, supported by several subcategories such as comprehension, apply reading skills, evaluate/interpret what is read, and attitude toward reading. Space also was provided for written comments. Students were graded on each subcategory in addition to their overall reading grade. The previously discussed observation data related well to the subcategories on these report cards and these data provided information for purposes of assessing students in several areas. We can illustrate this using Noelia's observation grid as an example (Figure 7). Her comments for indicators such as Uses Prior Knowledge to Make Meaning ("TV shows are so violent"), Relates to Personal Experience ("I got hit with a football and didn't get a black eye"), and Asks Questions to Further Understanding ("Wonder if Billy Ray was beating Alma before they got married?") could be used as evidence that she comprehended the book because she used her prior knowledge and personal experiences to help make meaning of what she read. Noelia knew when her understanding was not clear and she asked questions to clarify her understanding.

To assess Noelia's ability to apply reading skills, her comments for Draws Inferences ("I think Cracker knows but won't tell because he might be scared that if Billy Ray finds out Alma will get beaten more"), Makes Predictions ("Alma will go back to Billy Ray because she has so many times before"), Identifies Theme ("protecting your family"), Imagery, and Vocabulary could be used. The indicators related to character (e.g., Personally Identifies with Character; Evaluates Character) also could be used for this subcategory because character development is another common reading skill. These indicators are all reading skills and Noelia's observation data for each indicator provides evidence that she applied these skills as she read and discussed her book.

Observations from the indicator Questions the Author could be used as evidence for the subcategory "evaluate/interpret what is read" because students' comments in this indicator are often critiques of the book. This subcategory also could be addressed through comments from the Evaluates Character or Draws Inferences indicators, because students must be able to interpret what they are reading to make the appropriate inferences and evaluations. Marcy and I also used the students' comments from their observation charts in our written comments on the report card to illustrate to parents how their child was demonstrating the various literacy abilities. Parents appreciate these examples and find them helpful in understanding their child's reading development.

Determining what observation data support which subcategory on a student's report card still does not result in an actual letter grade, but the observation data provide information about what skills students are displaying during authentic, meaningful literacy tasks, and whether they are displaying these skills on a consistent basis. It is important to remember that our observation notes are only one form of assessment, and as Regie Routman (1994) reminds us, no single assessment tool can provide a comprehensive picture of a student's learning. A complete picture can only be formed by using a variety of measures that are examined over a period of time. Therefore, Marcy and I also used assessment measures such as end of book projects, independent practice activities from strategy lessons, running records, and whole-class read aloud discussion observations in our assessment of students. We did not have a nice, neat procedure for how we put all these different measures together to form a single letter grade. Rather, we looked over all the information we had for each of the subcategories on the report card and determined what letter grade would be appropriate for each subcategory. We then averaged the grades for the subcategories to generate the student's overall reading grade.

Although this process may seem more subjective than the traditional columns of workbook grades neatly averaged into a letter grade, it is based on strong evidence collected from numerous sources, and I believe it provides a much more accurate representation of what a student can do while engaging in real-life literacy activities. When parents came into our classroom to discuss their child's reading grade, they always were satisfied by the vast amount of information we could show them regarding their child's reading development (i.e., observation grids, literature logs, projects, running records). For additional ideas on how to create more specific guidelines for your evaluation process that are consistent with the constructivist theory guiding this book, see the sources in Box 5.1, particularly Chapter 13 from Regie Routman's *Invitations: Changing as Teachers and Learners K–12*.

BOX 5.1
Sources for Literacy Assessment

Paradis, E., Chatton, B., Boswell, A., Smith, M., & Yovich, S. (1991). Accountability: Assessing comprehension during literature discussion. *The Reading Teacher, 45,* 8–17.

Raphael, T.E., Pardo, L.S., Highfield, K., & McMahon, S.I. (1997). *Book club: A literature-based curriculum.* Littleton, MA: Small Planet Communications.

Routman, R. (1994). *Invitations: Changing as teachers and learners K–12.* Portsmouth, NH: Heinemann.

Watson, D. (1990). Show me: Whole language evaluation of literature groups. In K.G. Short & K.M. Pierce (Eds.), *Talking about books: Creating literate communities* (pp. 157–176). Portsmouth, NH: Heinemann.

Chapter 6

Social and Cultural Influences on Literature Discussions

Mrs. Evans! My new [discussion] group is all girls! I'm so excited!
It's going to be so much better than last time with boys. This is just going
to be the best!   *Kaitlyn*

Listening to the excitement in Kaitlyn's voice as she expressed these sentiments was a definite clue to me that literature discussion groups are about far more than just reading and talking about books. As teachers, we sometimes focus exclusively on the cognitive and academic aspects of activities. We plan for and design our instruction to provide students with opportunities to explore the world of literature in meaningful ways, and to help them develop skills that encourage a deeper appreciation of what they read. In our emphasis on cognitive learning it is easy to forget that literature discussions are inherently a social activity. Social and cultural factors (e.g., gender, race, power status) are present in these groups and have the potential to influence how our students experience their learning opportunities in such contexts. The focus of this chapter is to further explore the influence of social and cultural factors on students' literature discussions using students' own perceptions of how they feel these factors affect their experiences in discussion groups. If you thought planning for, implementing, and assessing literature discussion groups was complicated, it is about to become even more so.

Most of the examples of student discussions in this chapter come from the year I spent in Marcy's classroom. These discussion groups were videotaped, and students watched their videotapes the next day and reflected on how their discussions had gone. It was primarily through these group reflections that I gained insight into how students perceived the social and cultural factors influencing their discussions. In particular, Marcy's students felt that gender and "bossy people" (a form of power/status) were definite influences in how they experienced their literature discussions. The following sections present these students' voices as they explain their feelings about these two factors. The dilemmas the students' perceptions raised for Marcy and me, and the implications of these issues for us as teachers, also will be addressed.

Reflection Point 6.1

Take a minute and hypothesize how you think social and cultural factors might be influencing your students' discussion groups. Have your students given you any clues (such as Kaitlyn's comment) that issues such as gender, race, or power relations might affect what goes on in their groups?

Students' Perceptions of Gender

"Us Versus Them"

Noelia:	'Cause you can speak more [in all-girl groups]. With boys, the boys would be like, "oh whatever" (said sarcastically).
Amy:	Yeah. They wouldn't agree with you at all.
Jessie:	Even if you had like the same opinion and they had like the same thing, they would only agree on theirs even though they're the same thing. They wouldn't agree on ours.

Amy:	When I was [in a previous group] with Will, Pete, and Scott, they didn't agree on nothing that me and Tracey wanted to do.
Karen:	Why do you think that is?
Amy:	'Cause they want their way, probably.
Noelia:	Not only that, it's maybe some of the ideas they might think are girlish ones.
Amy:	And when you're talking, they just start butting in and they think they know what you're talking about but they really don't.

Students often used gender as an explanation for why their group was working well or having difficulties. This was particularly the case when talking with mixed-gender groups that were struggling. In these groups, students were quick to blame the other gender for their difficulties, and an "us versus them" mentality often became apparent. For example, in the *Great Gilly Hopkins* group, Jessie and Keely consistently did not read the book and refused to participate in the discussion, while Michael and Stan became increasingly frustrated at their inability to engage in a productive discussion due to the girls' overt refusal to read or discuss. When I asked the girls about the problems in the group, they said that the boys' attitude, rather than their own lack of participation, was the problem. Jessie told me,

> Michael has to have everything perfect, everyone has to read to just the right spot and have their journal and participate and if it's not perfect, you can't do anything. And Stan always takes Michael's side. We had read most of the [assignment] but Michael got mad because we hadn't read the whole thing.

I noted the us versus them mentality in other mixed-gender groups as well. After observing the *Monkey Island* group, I wrote the following in my journal:

> The *Monkey Island* group was a disaster today and fell along gender lines. When I asked them why they were having problems, the boys said it was because the girls only wanted to read their journals and then start reading the book; they didn't want to talk. The girls said it was because all the boys were doing was playing with their erasers. So, the boys blamed

the girls and the girls blamed the boys. The result, no discussion occurred and they simply separated into groups of two—one comprised of two girls and one with two boys.

It often appeared that regardless of the actual reason for the difficulties groups encountered (e.g., students not reading or not wanting to participate), the students focused on gender as the main reason for their group's problems. The problem was not that some group members were not reading or participating, it was that the *opposite gender* members were not reading or participating that became the most salient issue for the students. Even the students' nonverbal behavior communicated the us versus them mentality. In the mixed-gender groups that struggled, the girls sat on one side of the group, the boys sat on the other, and they often refused to look at each other. Videotapes were filled with glares and disgusted looks directed toward the other gender. It's important to point out that not all the mixed-gender groups encountered these types of difficulties—some worked well. When mixed-gender groups did struggle, however, students consistently blamed the other gender for their problems.

Multiple Perspectives and Gender

Although teachers often use discussion groups to encourage students' development of multiple perspectives and interpretations of literature, our students found that multiple perspectives can become problematic when the different perspectives are held by members of the other gender. The following student comments illustrate this problem:

Michael: It seems like girls and boys really have totally different opinions about things. And then it's kind of hard. I mean, it's O.K. to like, think differently, but, you know, that's part of what makes it harder.

Jessie: I think [*Cracker Jackson*] is better for all girls because boys, they would probably think the abuse, the violence, like, with Billy Ray hitting Alma, they would think that was cool because they're so into violent stuff and they would ruin the discussion for us because it's not cool.

Kaitlyn: Boys will go off on some subject and talk about sports or something. Like about the chapter, it's like, if they had

> sports in it, the boys would go onto sports like,"Oh look at Shaq [basketball player Shaquille O'Neal], isn't he cool?"
>
> **Amy:** That's what I'm afraid of, like, if you say something, the boys will just laugh at you, like they know everything you're gonna say.
>
> **Jessie:** Yeah, and then they'll start laughing and then your feelings are like kind of hurt because that's how you feel, that's your opinion.
>
> **Will:** I wasn't in any all-boy group but I think it'd be better 'cause when I was in another group, the boys want to talk about certain issues in books and girls want to talk about other issues and we had a little fighting that started.

Listening to comments such as these helped me to realize that the whole notion of multiple interpretations is not always as positive or straightforward as we may think. Marcy's students showed us that although multiple perspectives can lead to deeper understandings, they also have the potential to create barriers to discussion, especially when combined with gender issues. If students are fearful that other group members—particularly students of the other gender—will laugh at their opinions, there is little likelihood that they will view discussion groups as places where they can share and discuss their interpretations and personal feelings about what they read.

Research by Cherland (1992) offers another way to interpret Marcy's students' perceptions. Cherland argues that boys and girls use different types of discourse in their discussions. In her research with sixth-grade students, she found that girls tended to use a discourse of feeling while boys used a discourse of action. Cherland described a discourse of feeling as one that focuses on the emotion in the text, deals with human relationships, and values caring. In contrast, a discourse of action is concerned with logic, values reason and believability, and seeks meaning in the plot and action. If you think back to the excerpts of discussions shared in previous chapters, you can see evidence of these different types of discourse at work in Marcy's classroom. For example, the focus of the all-girl *Cousins* group discussion (Chapter 4, page 73) was the caring nature of families, the relationship between Patty Ann and her cousin Cammy, and how Patty Ann's mother treated Cammy after her daughter drowned. This discussion primarily used a discourse of feeling. In contrast, the all-boy *How to Get Fabulously Rich* group discussion (Chapter 3, page 40) focused on topics such as the believability of the story line (Could a child really win the lottery and how would he buy the ticket?), and ways to make the book more exciting (Someone tries to shoot the boy after he wins the money and this person goes to jail). This discussion mainly used a discourse of action.

One possible critique of Cherland's research is that it leads to the stereotyping of students and the types of talk found in discussions, because in many instances the discourse is not that clear cut. Girls also use discourses of action and boys use discourses of feeling. Moreover, a comparison of the two types of discourse can set up a potential hierarchy in which a discourse of action—with its emphasis on logic, believability, and plot—may be viewed as more intelligent, and consequently valued more, than a discourse that emphasizes feelings and caring.

Despite these potential caveats, the students' comments still provide evidence that girls and boys often want to talk about different topics in their discussions, that they have different responses to books, and that they interpret books in different ways. As educators, we need to be aware of these differences and be vigilant in our efforts to notice when differences create inequitable learning opportunities for our students. Marcy's students' fear of being laughed at underscores the need for us to strengthen our efforts to create classrooms and group contexts in which all students' opinions and ideas are valued, regardless of gender.

A Preference for Same-Gender Groups

Perhaps because of the problems encountered in many mixed-gender groups, students consistently told Marcy and me that they preferred to be placed in groups of the same gender. As we talked with students in their reflection discussions, the students offered convincing arguments as to why they viewed same-gender groups to be more conducive to their discussion and learning opportunities. One common reason offered was that students simply felt more comfortable around members of the same gender. Listen to what students in two different groups had to say about their experiences in a same-gender group. The first group was an all-boy group (*How to Get Fabulously Rich*), the second was an all-girl group (*Cracker Jackson*).

Group 1

Karen:	Why do you think your group is so effective?
Pete:	(immediately) It's all boys!
Karen:	Does that make a difference?
Pete:	Yeah, 'cause we're so used to talking to each other and so if like girls get in a group, you would really want to hang out with the boys instead of the girls. You don't hang out with girls!
Michael:	You don't hang out with girls a lot, you don't. It's different.
Brad:	We're just so used to talking and playing with boys.
Michael:	And I bet you could ask any all-girl group and they would probably say it's easier too.
Pete:	It's easier to contribute to the story with all boys 'cause it feels more comfortable.

Group 2

Jessie:	When you're in an all-girl group, it's easier.
Noelia:	That's why I think it would be better if all the boys were together and all the girls were together.
Amy:	'Cause you're not so shy around boys or something, if you are. I'm not.
Noelia:	Yeah, like I'm very outspoken around girls but if there's a boy around, I'm kind of shy.
Jessie:	Yeah, me too.
Noelia:	I mean, not shy where I won't talk but—
Amy:	Yeah, I mean, I can go up and talk to a guy but not as much as I can with a girl.
Noelia:	I think you feel more comfortable around girls because you're a girl and I bet the boys probably feel the same way about boys with boys.
Jessie:	And it's kind of easier even if it's like, girls you don't like because—
Noelia:	'Cause you're still all girls!
Jessie:	—like, even though you don't like them, you can still work with them 'cause they're still girls and everything and it's easier to talk to them.

Another reason offered by the students for their same-gender group preference was the fact that girls and boys are starting to "like" each other at this age. While talking with the *Shiloh* group about their all-girl experience, Keely said, "Maybe you like somebody in the group and you might feel embarrassed to talk. I know my friend is like that. If she likes someone, she won't even talk to 'em or talk around 'em." The *Cousins* group also addressed this issue specifically in their reflection discussion:

Kaitlyn:	And sometimes around boys, you gotta all admit, some of you get shy. You don't feel comfortable around boys.
Tracey:	And you really don't want to act stupid in front of them.
Daria:	Yeah, 'cause you're getting older and you start to like boys and you get uncomfortable around them.
Kaitlyn:	Boys are sometimes pretty immature, like, if you say something and they'll make fun of you and call you something, you know what I mean?
Regan:	I think it would make me not want to talk at all.
Daria:	Especially if you're nervous and you're in a group with boys and you like one of the boys in your group. 'Cause you're getting older and you're starting to like boys, but then you think, if someone makes fun of you and maybe he'll laugh at you and then you'll feel really more awful.

As revealed by these responses, at the heart of this issue was the fear that students would be laughed at or ridiculed by, or in front of, someone they "liked." Jessie's and Amy's earlier comments suggest that at least some girls were afraid of being laughed at by boys, and the *Cousin* group's conversation reveals that the issue of "liking someone" served to compound that fear. Interestingly, this fear of being laughed at was only talked about by girls. Although boys also often said they preferred same gender groups, they never discussed the possibility of being laughed at by girls.

I realize that the above perceptions could be viewed as stereotypical and serve only to reinforce gender stereotypes of girls as boy crazy, overly concerned with what others think of them, and apt to put their social lives ahead of their academic responsibilities. However, these students' perceptions raise questions about the need to feel safe while expressing ideas in literature discussion groups. Stereotypic or not, it was obvious that some girls in Marcy's class were worried about how boys would respond to their ideas and this led them to be cautious, or silent, participants in their discussions. Consequently, their opportunities for learning through engaging in literature discussions were compromised. Unfortunately, there is growing evidence that Marcy's students are not alone in their concerns. An increasing amount of research—both in literature discussion groups and other small-group contexts—reveals that girls are often disenfranchised and silenced, and their contributions are either ignored or devalued, by their male group members. For research that specifically addresses this concern, refer to the sources found in Box 6.1.

Box 6.1
Resources to Explore Gender Inequities in Literature Discussions and Small-Group Contexts

Alvermann, D.E. (1995). Peer-led discussions: Whose interests are served? *Journal of Adolescent & Adult Literacy, 39,* 282–289.

Evans, K.S. (1996). A closer look at literature discussion groups: The influence of gender on student response and discourse. *The New Advocate, 9*(3), 183–196.

Gallas, K. (1995). *Talking their way into science: Hearing children's questions and theories, responding with curricula.* New York: Teachers College Press.

Guzzetti, B., & Williams, W. (1996). Changing the pattern of gendered discussion: Lessons from science classrooms. *Journal of Adolescent & Adult Literacy, 40,* 38–47.

Moje, E., & Shepardson, D. (1998). Social interactions and children's changing understanding of electric circuits: Exploring unequal power relations in "peer"-learning groups. In B. Guzzetti & C. Hynd (Eds.), *Perspectives on conceptual change: Multiple ways to understand knowing and learning in a complex world* (pp. 225–234). Mahwah, NJ: Erlbaum.

It is difficult for us as teachers to know what to do about these concerns. On the one hand, it would be easy to simply allow students only to work in same-gender groups, but I am sure most educators would agree that this is not a viable solution. Students need to learn how to work with, and be respectful of, members of the opposite gender. By segregating our students, we run the risk of perpetuating, rather than altering, gender stereotypes. But the question remains, What do we do in response to the insights about gender shared with us by our students?

A first step is to recognize that gender does influence students' experiences and the learning opportunities available to them in literature discussion groups. Although the influence of gender issues may seem apparent after reading Marcy's students' thoughts, it is not always that easily recognizable. When I first began to share some of my findings regarding gender concerns, I received a wide variety of responses from other educators. In particular, I tried to discuss one group from Roxanne and Clay's classroom where I argued that Jonathan and the other boys were harrassing Mimi (see Evans, 1996, in Box 6.1, for a complete discussion of this group). The boys consistently called Mimi a dog, made barking noises whenever she tried to speak, and made comments such as "You should be in your doghouse. Why don't you come over to my house and eat some grass? Why are you talking? You're a dog—dogs don't talk." As the boys continued this behavior over several days, Mimi's reaction changed from striking back verbally and physically to simply accepting it and looking as if she were about to cry. Whereas I viewed this behavior as unacceptable harassment, others who read my account claimed that there was no gender-related issue and that this was merely typical "boy" behavior. I disagreed with the "boy behavior" interpretation, but this response helped me to realize that as educators, we need to be open to seeing how gender influences are at work in our classrooms, often in seemingly invisible ways.

Reflection Point 6.2

1. For the next several days, make a special effort to observe your classroom for possible gender-related influences. Specifically look for gender issues at work in your students' literature discussions.

2. Video- or audiotape two different discussion groups. If possible, tape a same-gender group and a mixed-gender group. As you watch the tapes, look and listen for things such as evidence of Cherland's discourse of feeling and discourse of action (i.e., what topics girls bring up for discussion, what topics boys bring up?), who asks the questions or assumes leadership positions, whose ideas are ignored and whose are elaborated on by others, who does the most talking and who is silent, and who gets

interrupted and who does the interrupting. Although these examples illustrate how boys can silence girls, be sure to also look for examples of girls silencing boys.

Recognizing that gender influences learning in our classrooms is only the first step; we must also take action to address this issue. Marcy and I routinely addressed the gender issues that students raised in their reflection discussions in our whole-class debriefing sessions. We tried to push students to explore the reasons and motivations behind what was happening in their groups, and to generate possible ways of dealing with the gender issues they experienced. Unfortunately, our efforts were largely in vain. Students clung to their belief that the way to"solve the gender problem"was to simply have same-gender groups. For the most part, we were unable to get students to move beyond this type of thinking. Although several students would say that they needed to learn to work with people of the other gender, there also was the unspoken belief that there was plenty of time to learn that later. Right now, they preferred same-gender groups. Their responses, however, only serve to reinforce my belief that we must continue in our efforts to help students examine the way gender operates in their lives, and push them to explore ways to address the gender issues they encounter both in and out of school.

Reflection Point 6.3

1. Using your observation notes from the previous reflection point, lead a discussion with your students to address their perceptions of how, or whether, gender influences their discussion experiences. Are they aware of gender issues at work in their discussion groups? If so, how would they like to address these issues? If not, how might you raise their awareness by using your observation notes as examples?

2. How do your students' comments compare to Marcy's students? Do they share her students' preference for same-gender groups?

Realizing that gender influences student participation and experience in literature discussion groups has implications for us as teachers with regard to our grouping practices. I know many teachers, myself included, who often unquestioningly put boys and girls together in small groups because there is the assumption that heterogeneous gender groups are the norm. When I initiate conversations with other teachers about their grouping practices, they often tell me that they would never have a group of all boys for fear of the resulting management problems. Listening to Marcy's students talk about their emphatic desire for same-gender groups—and their valid reasons for preferring such groups—along with my own observations of the effectiveness of the majority of same-gender groups (including the all-boy groups), pushed me to reexamine the assumption that we need to have mixed-gender discussion groups in our classrooms.

Again, I do not suggest that we should resort to having *only* same-gender groups. Quite the contrary, we should continue to encourage students to engage in meaningful discussions with classmates of the other gender, and help them explore the different types of responses and interpretations that are possible in such discussions. I raise this issue to explore, in a conscious and thoughtful way, the possibilities that exist in same-gender groups, and to encourage teachers to allow students to experience this arrangement when appropriate. One way to do this is to give students a choice in determining what book they read, because some books seem to appeal more to one gender or the other. This happened frequently in Marcy's classroom; only boys selected *How to Get Fabulously Rich* (Rockwell, 1991) as their first choice of books and only girls selected *Cousins* (Hamilton, 1990). In Marcy's classroom, we allowed for same-gender groups when they occurred due to student selections, and these were frequently the most productive, thoughtful, and meaningful discussion groups we observed. Rather than feeling pressured to place both boys and girls in each group merely for the sake of having a heterogeneous gender mix, I began to realize the benefits that exist when these same-gender groups are allowed to arise naturally through the students' own selections. There are no easy answers to this issue, but based on what I have seen and heard, I believe that there is a need for educators to thoughtfully consider gender issues when forming literature discussion groups in classrooms.

Reflection Point 6.4

How do you group your students for literature discussions? Is the gender composition of the group a consideration for you? What possible assumptions do you have regarding gender and grouping practices? How might you begin to examine those assumptions in light of what you have read here?

Students' Perceptions of "Bossy People"

> If only one person does all the talking, you just get sick of hearing their voice.
>
> Ethan

In addition to gender, students brought up the social factor of "bossy people" and the impact such group members had on their discussions. If students perceived a member of their group to be bossy, they consistently said that they disliked the way that person behaved and viewed it as a negative influence on their own behavior, as well as on the discussion. I asked students to explain how such people influenced their group, and they responded:

Noelia: She just has to be the whole big person of it, like I'm the manager or I'm the boss and you listen to me because this is what we're gonna do. In [my group] she'd sit and go, "Oh Noelia, that's not even right" and so I just got up and walked out 'cause I felt so embarrassed.... I think bossy people are a problem because they talk the most and they don't give anyone else a chance to talk.

Jessie: They're not gonna [let you] talk about anything; it's like they're always hogging everything and you can't get to say anything because they talk too long.

Keely: They're always telling us what to do, and just reading out of their journal and not giving us a chance.

Hannah: He wouldn't let us read. He kept reading and reading until the whole book was finished. If you tried [to read] he would just keep going and make you stop.

Regan:	They boss you around and you don't get to hear what other people think because they won't let anybody else talk.... They make others not want to talk or read.
Kari:	They make you not like lit groups.
Amy:	In [my group] it was really hard to cooperate with [bossy student] because she'd just like, read her journal and then she'd go, "you go, then you go," and I don't like it when people do that to me.... And like when somebody was talking and then they just start interrupting you when you're in the middle of something and that bothers you because I want to share what I was saying and they interrupt me.

You can hear in these students' voices that bossy people influenced their discussion in numerous ways—all negative. They controlled who talked and who did not, interrupted people when others tried to talk, and dominated the discussion. As Noelia's comment revealed, they also tried to maintain control over whose interpretations were valued and deemed correct and whose were wrong. In some ways, these bossy group members were assuming the authoritarian role reserved for teachers in the traditional I-R-E discussion pattern (Cazden, 1986). In this pattern, the teacher initiates a discussion by asking a question (I), a student responds with an answer (R), and the teacher evaluates whether the response was correct (E). Given that a goal of literature discussions is to move away from teacher-controlled discussions and broaden the possibilities for multiple interpretations and perspectives, this constraint of the talk by an authoritarian student is problematic. As can be seen in Regan's and Kari's comments, this type of controlling behavior often resulted in students not enjoying their discussion experience.

Being Bossy Isn't the Same as Being a Leader

After students began discussing the impact of bossy members on their discussion groups, I observed these "bossy" students more closely when I sat in with their groups. Many of the behaviors they exhibited also could have been interpreted as leader-type behaviors. For instance, they often read their literature log first, they directed other people to read their log next, they asked people questions, and often they responded to what was said. It appeared that in many ways these students were acting like the leader (or perhaps the teacher?) in their discussion groups. I asked students about this when they brought up the bossy issue in their reflection discussions, and they were quick to point out that there were definite differences between a leader and someone who was bossy. I particularly asked the *How to Get Fabulously Rich* group about this distinction because Michael was obviously the leader of the group and the other boys even referred to him as the leader.

Karen:	Do you think your group has a leader?
Jalil:	Yeah, Michael.
Pete:	He does most of the talking, he gets the conversation started.
Karen:	So Michael helps your group by getting you started. Is that alright to have someone in your group who does that? (general agreement). How is that different from having a bossy member in your group?
Pete:	A bossy member tells you what to do and stuff and how to do it and stuff.
Karen:	So if you have someone in your group who tries to keep the group on task, is that being bossy?
Michael:	Not if they're responsible probably. If they're responsible, then they're probably respectful.
Will:	It would depend on how bossy they were. If it were like, "you go first and then I'll go and then after we're done we're reading to this page," that would bother me. But if they said, "alright, why don't you start, then me," then that would be OK.
Michael:	I think a leader shouldn't say you *have* to go [take your turn]. It's more of a type of a question, do you *want* to go? And usually the leader is more [to help keep the discussion going] but not necessarily bossy about it.

As this group demonstrated, the difference between being perceived as bossy and being perceived as a leader seemed to be *how* students enacted the leader-type behaviors rather than the actual behaviors themselves. Students were perceived as a leader if they made suggestions, asked students to participate, and used a respectful tone of voice, but they were considered bossy if they told people what to do, demanded participation, and used an overbearing tone of voice. It was not so much the behaviors themselves, but rather the manner students used when engaging in particular behaviors that determined how they were perceived.

Interestingly, the behaviors that bossy students exhibit are what we, as teachers, often hope to see our students doing in discussions. They read their literature journal, ask questions, facilitate discussion, and are active participants in the discussion process. Ironically, though, by engaging in the very behaviors that we encourage, these students actually end up being perceived in a negative way by members of their group. Marcy's students pointed to respect as being an important element in distinguishing between a bossy person and a leader. If a person was respectful while engaging in leader-type behaviors then that was acceptable, but if he or she was not respectful, these same behaviors became negative influences on the group.

Respect is undoubtedly an important part of this whole "bossy" issue, but I suspect that it also might have something to do with power issues within the discussion groups. By this I mean to consider the often-unexamined processes we use to form discussion groups. When I first started using literature discussion groups in my classroom, I allowed students to select their top three choices of texts and I used those choices to create the groups. However, I often found myself looking at the emerging configurations to see if a strong student was in each group—someone who would help to lead the group in a direction I thought appropriate. I was operating under the assumption that every group needed a leader-type person to help it run smoothly. In reflecting on this unconscious grouping practice, I realize that I may have been influenced by research on cooperative learning groups that often calls for the assignment of a group leader (Johnson, Johnson, & Holubec, 1990). Because literature discussion groups are a variation of cooperative learning groups, it is possible that our knowledge and assumptions about cooperative learning influence how we plan for and implement discussion groups.

Listening to Marcy's students has helped me to reexamine my assumptions about group leaders, especially because many of the most effective discussion groups were those where no single student assumed a leadership role. The students also commented on this phenomenon, saying that the best groups were those where no one person was a leader, but where all students had a chance to lead the discussion. In their reflection, *The Great Gilly Hopkins* group discussed this issue.

> **Jessie:** [If there's no leader], then maybe they won't be fighting or saying that they can just rule the whole thing or talk the whole time without anyone else.
>
> **Michael:** It makes everyone equal.
>
> **Karen:** Why is that important?
>
> **Stan:** It makes it easier to talk.
>
> **Michael:** Because you don't want one person talking a lot more than another one. So everybody's in the discussion.

Other students echoed this group's desire for everyone to assume a leader-type role and for everyone to be equal in a discussion group. Those students who had experienced having a bossy member in a group were even more adamant that groups were more effective without a leader. It was almost as if they would prefer to not have a leader because having a leader was one step closer to a person taking over and becoming bossy.

This does not mean that we should completely abandon the idea of having students assume leadership roles in their discussion groups. In fact, other students in Marcy's class advocated the need for having a leader in their group. In reflecting on this issue in a whole-class discussion, Scott explained why having a leader, or someone to take the initiative in starting the discussion, was helpful.

> 'Cause if you don't read [your journal], everybody's like scared to go. You ask one person to go, they're like, "no I'll go last" and it keeps going around. And if you tell someone, "you go next and then I'll go" or something like that, [that's better]. I never had no bossy [person] be in my group. Like me and Ethan, when we're in a group we ask somebody to read and, if they don't, then one of us two will read and then it's like somebody to guide you, not tell you what to do. Like you ask "do you want to read in your journal first?" or if it's not that, then nobody's reading or everybody's just sitting there.

Pete agreed when he described his experience in the *How to Get Fabulously Rich* group (who all perceived Michael to be the leader). He said, "In one of our groups, we kind of wanted somebody to lead. One time [Michael] was gone and it wasn't as exciting. We all wanted him back."

Consequently, students were not willing to unilaterally categorize leaders as a bad feature of discussion groups. As Scott's response indicates, however, even in advocating for a leader students were quick to clarify that they did not want a bossy leader.

So where does that leave us as teachers? Should we have leaders or not have leaders? Should we allow students to select their group leaders or have teachers assign them? As with most dilemmas in education, there are no easy answers and no one answer is appropriate for every discussion group. As Marcy's students' perceptions indicate, this is not a question that can be answered with a yes or no response. Some groups—like the *Cousins*, *Shiloh*, and *Cracker Jackson* groups—worked wonderfully without a leader, while other groups like the *How to Get Fabulously Rich* group benefited from and enjoyed having someone assume the leader role. Still other groups, such as *The Great Gilly Hopkins* group, had students who tried to assume a leadership role but wound up being perceived as bossy.

Marcy and I addressed this issue by deciding not to assign leaders for our discussion groups. This was largely due to our observations of various groups at work, which helped us to see the difficulties that students encountered when a leader stepped over the bounds and became bossy. The other students perceived the bossy leader as imposing ideas and procedures on them, and we felt that by assigning a leader we would be encouraging this sense of imposition. We saw numerous groups in which there was no leader and the group worked fine, so we knew that having a leader was not necessary for having a productive discussion group. We let groups decide for themselves if they needed a leader or not. For the most part, the groups seemed to be able to determine if they needed guidance and in those cases, a group member, or members, stepped up and assumed that role.

It was in the groups where the members did not want a leader, but someone still tried to assume the role, that issues of bossiness arose. This was the type of situation that Marcy and I focused on in our efforts to deal with the leader/bossy issue. As with the gender concerns, we consistently addressed the issue with students both in their reflection discussions and in whole-class debriefings. By bringing this topic into the open for discussion, we hoped to help students continue to refine their views of leaders and bossy people and to encourage them to reflect on their own behavior in discussion groups. We emphasized the need for respect and tried to help students see how it is the *way* someone talks, rather than what they actually say, that determines whether they are perceived as a helpful leader or as a bossy person. For the most part, these types of discussions seemed to help because by the end of the year, we were only hearing complaints about bossiness related to one particular student in the class, Daria, which Marcy chose to address individually with her.

Reflection Point 6.5

1. Go back to the discussions you audio- or videotaped for Reflection Point 6.2. Watch or listen to them again, and this time pay particular attention to issues of leadership and power. Some possible things to look for might be, How does power get distributed in the groups? Do group members share the power and leadership responsibilities or does a certain student assume that role? Do you see evidence of bossiness? How does having a leader or bossy member appear to influence the group's discussion and other students' participation?

2. Lead another discussion with your class regarding these issues. What are their perceptions? How might you use their perceptions, along with your observations, to rethink your grouping practices and possible assumptions regarding leadership roles in small-group contexts?

Bossiness and Gender Issues

Just as Marcy and I were beginning to think we had sufficiently addressed the bossy issue, we heard Michael make the following comment:

> It seems like some of the girls in this class just wanna be boss. They snap their fingers and stuff, they just do what they want to do, when they want to do it.... But, that's just an opinion. The girls would say that the boys would be bossy but the boys would say the girls would be bossy.

Michael's comment, made late in the school year, provided me with another way to interpret how the bossy issue was influencing the discussion groups: I started to wonder if the bossy issue was somehow connected to gender issues. I went back through my observation notes and discovered that all the groups that had complained of bossy members were heterogenous-gender groups. There was not a single instance in a same-gender group in which students encountered problems relating to a bossy group member. Furthermore, in the mixed-gender groups it was usually one gender accusing someone of the other gender of being bossy. It was as if the boys and girls were on teams, with each gender fighting for power. For example, in *The Great Gilly Hopkins* group, Jessie and Keely consistently accused Michael of being bossy and trying to control the group, and also accused Stan of siding with Michael. To me, Michael's behavior seemed appropriate and merely an attempt to get the group to work, but the girls viewed him as a controlling and negative influence. Once again, it appeared that it was not so much that a group member was trying to draw Jessie and Keely into the discussion or encourage them to do the reading that was troublesome to them, but rather it was the fact that it was someone of the *opposite gender* doing those things that bothered them. There was another girl in the group who also tried to get Jessie and Keely to keep up with the reading and they did not perceive her to be bossy. Ironically, the boys in the group did—even though she was trying to get the girls to do the same thing that Michael was. Bossiness here was not only a matter of how the behaviors were enacted (i.e., the respect issue), but it also was influenced by the gender of the person enacting the behaviors and the gender of the student at whom the behaviors were directed.

It was not always an "us versus them" situation, however, and there were times when students of the same gender considered each other to be bossy. If you look back at the students' comments on page 126–127, both Noelia's and Amy's comments referred to another girl in the class— Daria. Daria was overbearing in her discussion groups and often tried to control the groups overtly. She directed who could talk when and who could read their literature log. She also dominated the discussion by sharing long, detailed personal stories, and she frequently interrupted people. It would be hard to imagine anyone interpreting her behavior as anything but bossy, regardless of gender. I believe that there is a gender connection in Daria's behavior, however, due to what I observed during the last literature cycle. Before this cycle, Daria had only been a member of mixed-gender groups and her behavior was consistently bossy. In the last cycle, however, she was placed in the all-girl *Cousins* group and it was as if I was watching a different person. None of the bossy behaviors that occurred continually in her previous groups appeared here. In comparison to the demanding, long-winded group member of the past, in the *Cousins* group she let others talk freely, responded without interrupting, and never tried to take over the discussion. Although I'm sure there are other possible explanations for the change in her behavior, I have to wonder if it was due in part to the same-gender composition of her group.

Where Am I Now? Remaining Unanswered Questions

A jumble of new questions were raised for me as I looked at my discussion groups through the lenses of gender and power issues. For instance, what is it about mixed-gender groups that prompts some students to engage in such overt bossy behavior? Why does the fight for power seem to be less of an issue in same-gender groups? I do not have an answer to these questions and I doubt a definitive one exists. Listening to and watching Marcy's students closely, however, has helped me to better understand Vygotsky's sociocultural theory that advocates studying contexts holistically and in all their complexity, rather than reducing them into separate elements to be studied in isolation. In other words, exploring the mutual influence of bossy members and gender in Marcy's classroom allowed me to begin to see that social and cultural factors do not occur in a vacuum. Rather, they interact with each other and mutually influence the learning context. It is not enough to attend to matters of power and gender—or to other social and cultural factors such as language, religion, ethnicity, and economic background—in isolation. We can explore such factors individually as a place to start, but to truly understand the complexity of literature discussion groups we also must be willing to explore how these factors interrelate to influence students' experiences and perceptions.

When we add social and cultural issues to the academic concerns that are our main focus as teachers, we discover an amazingly complex phenomenon. Although it may seem like a daunting task to consider all these factors when working with literature discussion groups, I prefer to see it as an exciting journey that is filled with unexpected turns and detours. I do not think that reaching the destination (or the answer to all the dilemmas raised in this book) is the most important part of the journey. Rather, I think it is most important that we listen closely to what our students are telling us as we continue to explore the complex learning context of literature discussion groups. The one thing of which I am certain is that we will never understand the complexity of these groups without keeping our students clearly and consciously in sight. Their perspectives are sure to lead us to exciting, new, and unanticipated possibilities.

Reflection Point 6.6

Look back to the list of questions, challenges, and possibilities that you generated in the beginning of this book.

1. What possible ideas or answers have you found here to address your challenges and questions?

2. What evidence have you found to suggest your possibilities can become realities?

3. What new questions and possibilities have been generated for you that will guide your future work in exploring the use of literature discussion groups in your classroom?

List of Discussion Topics

Possible things to discuss in your literature group:

1. Relate the book to your own experiences.
2. Make predictions.
3. Use the book to support your predictions or opinions.
4. Describe what people/places/things in the book look like.
5. Share how a character is like/not like you.
6. Evaluate a character.
7. Compare a character in the book to a character from another book you have read.
8. Describe what you would do if you were in the story.
9. Question the author.
10. Relate or compare the book to another book you have read.
11. Relate or compare the book to a movie or television show you have seen.
12. Ask questions to further your understanding of the book.
13. Retell or summarize a portion of the book.
14. Identify the theme of the book.
15. Ask about unknown words in the book.
16. Explain how the story would be different if another person/character were telling it.
17. Share any interesting language the author used.

Appendix B

Story Map With Character Perspectives Sheet

Book Being Read _____

Group Members _____

Main character's perspective—how she/he feels	Important events in the story	Second character's perspective—how she/he feels

Student Self- and Peer-Assessment Form

Literature Group Evaluation   Name_____

Book_____

Group Members	Rating	Reason
1. Yourself		
2.		
3.		
4.		
5.		
6.		

Scale: +Excellent   ✔+Really Good   ✔O.K.   ✔–Needs Improvement   –Not Acceptable

Appendix D

Observation Grid

Uses prior knowledge to make meaning	Relates to personal experience	Makes predictions	Uses text to support predictions	Imagery
Personally identifies with a character	Evaluates character	Places self in story	Questions the author	Connects to other texts
Asks questions to further understanding	Draws inferences	Elaborates on others' comments	Retells/Summarizes	Identifies theme
Vocabulary/Uses	Materials: Book- Read- Response Log-		Miscellaneous	

References

Allen, A. (1997). Creating spaces for discussions about social justice and equity in an elementary classroom. *Language Arts*, 74(4), 518–524.

Allen, J. (1999). *Words, words, words: Teaching vocabulary in grades 4–12*. York, ME: Stenhouse.

Alvermann, D.E. (1995). Peer-led discussions: Whose interests are served? *Journal of Adolescent & Adult Literacy*, 39, 282–289.

Apple, M., & Beane, J. (1995). *Democratic schools*. Alexandria, VA: Association for Supervision and Curriculum Development.

Beach, R., & Anson, C. (1993). Using peer-dialogue journals to foster response. In G.E. Newell & R.K. Durst (Eds.), *Exploring texts: The role of discussion and writing in the teaching and learning of literature*. Norwood, MA: Christopher-Gordon.

Blachowicz, C., & Lee, J. (1991). Vocabulary development in the whole literacy classroom. *The Reading Teacher*, 45, 188–195.

Blair-Larsen, S.M., & Williams, K.A. (Eds.). (1999). *The balanced reading program: Helping all students achieve success*. Newark, DE: International Reading Association.

Braunger, J., & Lewis, J.P. (1997). *Building a knowledge base in reading*. Newark, DE: International Reading Association; Portland, OR: Northwest Regional Educational Laboratory; Urbana, IL: National Council of Teachers of English.

Braunger, J., & Lewis, J.P. (1999). *Using the knowledge base in reading: Teachers at work*. Newark, DE: International Reading Association; Portland, OR: Northwest Regional Educational Laboratory.

Cazden, C.B. (1986). Classroom discourse. In M.C. Wittrock (Ed.), *Handbook of research on teaching* (3rd ed., pp. 432–463). New York: Macmillan.

Cherland, J., & Edelsky, C. (1993). Girls and reading: The desire for agency and the horror of helplessness in fictional encounters. In L. Christian-Smith (Ed.), *Texts of desire: Essays on fiction, femininity and schooling*. Washington, DC: The Falmer Press.

Commeyras, M. (1994). Were Janell and Neesie in the same classroom? Children's questions as the first order of reality in storybook discussions. *Language Arts*, 71(7), 517–523.

Daniels, H. (1994). *Literature circles: Voice and choice in the student-centered class-room.* York, ME: Stenhouse.

Davies, B. (1993). *Shards of glass: Children reading and writing beyond gendered identities.* Cresskill, NJ: Hampton Press.

Dewey, J. (1938). *Experience & education.* New York: Collier Books.

Dugan, J. (1997). Transactional literature discussions: Engaging students in the appreciation and understanding of literature. *The Reading Teacher, 51,* 4–29.

Eeds, M., & Wells, D. (1989). Grand conversations: An exploration of meaning construction in literature study groups. *Research in the Teaching of English, 23*(1), 4–29.

Emery, D. (1996). Helping readers comprehend stories from the characters' perspectives. *The Reading Teacher, 49,* 534–541.

Emery, D., & Mihalevich, C. (1992). Directed discussion of character perspectives. *Reading Research and Instruction, 31,* 51–59.

Evans, K.S. (1996). A closer look at literature discussion groups: The influence of gender on student response and discourse. *The New Advocate, 9*(3), 183–196.

Farest, C., & Miller, C. (1993). Children's insights into literature: Using dialogue journals to invite literary response. In D.J. Leu & C.K. Kinzer (Eds.), *Examining central issues in literacy research, theory, and practice. Forty-second yearbook of the National Reading Conference* (pp. 271–278). Chicago: National Reading Conference.

Fisher, P., Blachowicz, C., & Smith, J. (1991). Vocabulary learning in literature discussion groups. In J. Zutell & S. McCormick (Eds.), *Learner factors/teacher factors: Issues in literacy research and instruction. Fortieth yearbook of the National Reading Conference* (pp. 201–209). Chicago: National Reading Conference.

Fitzgerald, J. (1999). What is this thing called "balance?" *The Reading Teacher, 53,* 100–107.

Fitzgerald, J., & Spiegel, D.L. (1983). Enhancing children's reading comprehension through instruction in narrative structure. *Journal of Reading Behavior, 15,* 1–18.

Flitterman-King, S. (1988). The role of the response journal in active reading. *The Quarterly of the National Writing Project and the Center for the Study of Writing, 10,* 4–11.

Galda, L., Rayburn, S., & Stanzi, L.C. (2000). *Looking through the faraway end: Creating a literature-based reading curriculum with second graders.* Newark, DE: International Reading Association.

Gallas, K. (1995). *Talking their way into science: Hearing children's questions and theories, responding with curricula.* New York: Teachers College Press.

Goodman, Y. (1978). Kidwatching: An alternative to testing. *National Elementary Principal, 57,* 41–45.

Guzzetti, B., & Williams, W. (1996). Changing the pattern of gendered discussion: Lessons from science classrooms. *Journal of Adolescent & Adult Literacy, 40,* 38–47.

Hancock, M. (1993). Exploring and extending personal response through literature journals. *The Reading Teacher, 46*, 466–474.

Harste, J.C., Short, K.G., & Burke, C. (1988). *Creating classrooms for authors: The reading writing connection*. Portsmouth, NH: Heinemann.

Idol, L. (1987). Group story mapping: A comprehension strategy for both skilled and unskilled readers. *Journal of Learning Disabilities, 20*(4), 196–205.

Johnson, D., Johnson, R., & Holubec, E. (1990). *Circles of learning: Cooperation in the classroom*. Edina, MN: Interaction Books.

Kelly, P., & Farnan, N. (1991). Promoting critical thinking through response logs: A reader-response approach with fourth graders. In J. Zutell & S. McCormick (Eds.), *Learner factors/teacher factors: Issues in literacy research and instruction. Fortieth yearbook of the National Reading Conference*. Chicago: National Reading Conference.

Manzo, A., & Manzo, U. (1997). *Content area literacy: Interactive teaching for active learning*. Upper Saddle River, NJ: Merrill/Prentice-Hall.

Martinez, M.G., Roser, N.L., Hoffman, J.V., & Battle, J. (1992). Fostering better book discussions through response logs and a response framework: A case description. In C.K. Kinzer & D.J. Leu (Eds.), *Literacy research, theory, and practice: Views from many perspectives. Forty-first yearbook of the National Reading Conference*. Chicago: National Reading Conference.

McConaughy, S.H. (1980). Using story structure in the classroom. *Language Arts, 57*, 157–165.

Mitchell Pierce, K. (1988). Talking about books: An illustration with "Petronella." In C. Weaver, *Reading process and practice: From socio-psycholinguistics to whole language* (2nd ed., pp. 397–411). Portsmouth, NH: Heinemann.

Moje, E., & Shepardson, D. (1998). Social interactions and children's changing understanding of electric circuits: Exploring unequal power relations in "peer"-learning groups. In B. Guzzetti & C. Hynd (Eds.), *Perspectives on conceptual change: Multiple ways to understand knowing and learning in a complex world* (pp. 225–234). Mahwah, NJ: Erlbaum.

O'Flahavan, J. (1994/1995). Teacher role options in peer discussions about literature. *The Reading Teacher, 48*, 354–356.

Paley, V. (1986). On listening to what children say. *Harvard Educational Review, 56*, 122–131.

Paradis, E., Chatton, B., Boswell, A., Smith, M., & Yovich, S. (1991). Accountability: Assessing comprehension during literature discussion. *The Reading Teacher, 45*, 8–17.

Raphael, T.E. (1986). Teaching question answer relationships, revisited. *The Reading Teacher, 39*, 561–522.

Raphael, T.E., & McMahon, S.I. (1994). Book Club: An alternative framework for reading instruction. *The Reading Teacher, 48*, 102–116.

Raphael, T.E., Pardo, L.S., Highfield, K., & McMahon, S.I. (1997). *Book club: A literature-based curriculum*. Littleton, MA: Small Planet Communications.

Readence, J.E., Bean, T.W., & Baldwin, R.S. (1998). *Content area literacy: An integrated approach* (6th ed.). Dubuque, IA: Kendall/Hunt.

Richardson, V., Anders, P., Tidwell, D., & Lloyd, C. (1991). The relationship between beliefs and practices in reading comprehension instruction. *American Educational Research Journal, 28*(3), 559–586.

Rosenblatt, L. (1978). *The reader, the text, and the poem: The transactional theory of literary work.* Carbondale, IL: Southern Illinois University Press.

Roser, N.L., & Martinez, M.G. (1995). *Book talk and beyond: Children and teachers respond to literature.* Newark, DE: International Reading Association.

Routman, R. (1994). *Invitations: Changing as teachers and learners K–12.* Portsmouth, NH: Heinemann.

Rupley, W., Logan, J., & Nichols, W. (1998/1999). Vocabulary instruction in a balanced reading program. *The Reading Teacher, 52,* 336–346.

Shanahan, T., & Shanahan, S. (1997). Character perspective charting: Helping children to develop a more complete conception of story. *The Reading Teacher, 50,* 668–677.

Short, K.G., & Kauffman, G. (1992). Hearing students' voices: The role of reflection in learning. *The Whole Language Newsletter, 11*(3), 1–6.

Short, K.G., & Pierce, K. (1990). *Talking about books: Creating literate communities.* Portsmouth, NH: Heinemann.

Simpson, A. (1996). Critical questions: Whose questions? *The Reading Teacher, 50,* 118–127.

Spiegel, D.L. (1998). Silver bullets, babies, and bath water: Literature response groups in a balanced literacy program. *The Reading Teacher, 52,* 114–125.

Staal, L. (2000). The story face: An adaptation of story mapping that incorporates visualization and discovery learning to enhance reading and writing. *The Reading Teacher, 54,* 26–31.

Temple, C. (1993). What if Beauty had been ugly? Reading against the grain of gender bias in children's books. *Language Arts, 70*(2), 89–93.

Tierney, R.J., & Readence, J.E. (2000). *Reading strategies and practices: A compendium* (5th ed.). Boston: Allyn & Bacon.

Vygotsky, L.S. (1978). *Mind in society: The development of higher psychological processes.* (M. Cole, V.J. Steiner, S. Scribner, & E. Souberman, Eds. and Trans.). Cambridge, MA: Harvard University Press. (Original work published 1934)

Watson, D. (1990). Show me: Whole language evaluation of literature groups. In K.G. Short & K.M. Pierce (Eds.), *Talking about books: Creating literate communities* (pp. 157–176). Portsmouth, NH: Heinemann.

Weaver, C. (Ed.). (1998). *Reconsidering a balanced approach to reading.* Urbana, IL: National Council of Teachers of English.

Whitin, D., & Whitin, P. (1998). Learning is born of doubting: Cultivating a skeptical stance. *Language Arts, 76*(2), 123–129.

Wiencek, J., & O'Flahavan, J. (1994). From teacher-led to peer discussions about literature: Suggestions for making the shift. *Language Arts, 71*(7), 488–498.

Wollman-Bonilla, J., & Werchadlo, B. (1995). Literature response journals in a first-grade classroom. *Language Arts, 72*(8), 562–570.

Children's and Young Adult Literature References

Adler, D. (1992). *A picture book of Harriet Tubman*. New York: Scholastic.

Babbitt, N. (1975). *Tuck everlasting*. New York: The Trumpet Club.

Blume, J. (1980). *Superfudge*. New York: Dell.

Bunting, E. (1989). *The Wednesday surprise*. New York: Clarion.

Bunting, E. (1991). *Sharing Susan*. New York: HarperCollins.

Bunting, E. (1996). *The blue and the gray*. New York: Scholastic.

Byars, B.C. (1985). *Cracker Jackson*. New York: Viking.

Byars, B.C. (1985). *Goodbye, Chicken Little*. New York: Scholastic.

Cannon, J. (1993). *Stellaluna*. New York: Harcourt Brace.

Choi, S.N. (1991). *Year of impossible goodbyes*. New York: Dell.

Cleary, B. (1991). *Strider*. Ill. P.O. Zelinsky. New York: William Morrow.

Coerr, E. (1977). *Sadako and the thousand paper cranes*. New York: Harper & Row.

Cooney, C. (1991). *Face on the milk carton*. New York: Laurel Leaf.

dePaola, T. (1979). *Oliver Button is a sissy*. New York: Harcourt Brace Jovanovich.

Fox, P. (1991). *Monkey Island*. New York: Orchard.

Hamilton, V. (1990). *Cousins*. New York: Philomel.

Hess, K. (1992). *Letters from Rifka*. New York: Henry Holt.

Hoestlandt, J. (1993). *Star of fear, star of hope*. New York: Walker.

Hoffman, M. (1991). *Amazing Grace*. New York: Scholastic.

Hopkins, D. (1993). *Sweet Clara and the freedom quilt*. New York: Alfred A. Knopf.

Lowry, L. (1989). *Number the stars*. New York: Dell.

Lowry, L. (1993). *The giver*. New York: Bantom Doubleday Dell.

Myers, W.D. (1988). *Scorpions*. New York: HarperCollins.

Naylor, P.R. (1991). *Shiloh*. New York: Bantam Doubleday Dell.

Paterson, K. (1978). *The great Gilly Hopkins*. New York: The Trumpet Club.

Perl, L., & Lazan, M.B. (1996). *Four perfect pebbles: A Holocaust story*. New York: Scholastic.

Pettit, J. (1993). *A place to hide. True stories of Holocaust rescue*. New York: Scholastic.

Polacco, P. (1994). *Pink and Say*. New York: Philomel.

Reiss, J. (1972). *The upstairs room*. New York: Harper & Row.

Ringold, F. (1992). *Aunt Harriet's Underground Railroad*. New York: Scholastic.

Rockwell, T. (1973). *How to eat fried worms*. New York: Bantam Doubleday Dell.

Rockwell, T. (1991). *How to get fabulously rich*. New York: Yearling.

Rylant, C. (1985). A bad road for cats. In C. Rylant, *Every living thing*. New York: Aladdin.

Scieszka, J. (1989). *The true story of the three little pigs*. New York: Scholastic.

Sebestyen, O. (1979). *Words by heart*. Boston: Little, Brown.

Smith, R.K. (1972). *Chocolate fever*. New York: Bantam Doubleday Dell.

Smith, R.K. (1984). *The war with grandpa*. New York: Yearling.

Turner, A. (1987). *Nettie's trip south*. New York: Macmillan.

van Allsburg, C. (1993). *The sweetest fig*. Boston: Houghton Mifflin.

Voigt, C. (1981). *Homecoming*. New York: Ballantine.

Winter, J. (1988). *Follow the drinking gourd*. New York: Alfred A. Knopf.

Yashima, T. (1955). *Crow boy*. New York: Puffin Books.

Index

Page references followed by *b*, *f*, or *t* indicate boxes, figures, or tables, respectively.

A

Adler, D., 32*b*, 145
aesthetic reading, 20; Reflection Points, 21
Allen, A., 63*b*, 141
Allen, J., 82*b*, 141
Almasi, J.F., 25*b*
Alvermann, D.E., 122*b*, 141
Anders, P., 6, 143
Anson, C., 46*b*, 141
Apple, M., 11, 141
assessment(s): criteria for, 90–91, 91*t*; of discussion groups, 88–113; vs grading, 102–104; honesty in, 99–102; as learned process, 92–96; measures for, 112; peer assessments, 90–92, 93*f*, 96–99; Reflection Points for, 89–90, 102–104; role of student voice in, 96–99; self-assessments, 90–92, 96–99; sources for, 113*b*; student, 99–102; teacher, 104–110

B

Babbitt, N., 29, 145
"A Bad Road for Cats" (Rylant), 70
balanced reading programs, 68*b*
Baldwin, R.S., 46*b*, 143
Battle, J., 43, 51*b*, 143
Beach, R., 46*b*, 141
Bean, T.W., 11, 46*b*, 143
Beane, J., 141
Blachowicz, C., 82*b*, 141–142
Blair-Larsen, S.M., 68*b*, 141
Blume, J., 31*b*, 145
Book Club, 24–26

BOOKS: *Children's Choices* (International Reading Association), 30–35; for Civil War discussions, 32, 32*b*; for discussion groups, 31, 31*b*; read-aloud, 79–80; selection of, 30–35; for strategy lessons on theme, 84*b*; for World War II discussions, 32, 32*b*

"BOSSY PEOPLE," 115, 132–134; influence on groups, 126–127; vs leaders, 127–132; student perceptions of, 126–134

BOSWELL, A., 113*b*, 143

BRAUNGER, J., 68*b*, 141

BUNTING, E., 31*b*, 32*b*, 84*b*, 145

BURKE, C., 46*b*, 142

BYARS, B.C., 31*b*, 85, 145; *Cracker Jackson,* 47–48, 106, 106*f,* 120–121

C

CANNON, J., 84*b*, 145

CAZDEN, C.B., 127, 141

CDGS. *See* Conversational Discussion Groups

CHARACTER PERSPECTIVES, 68–77; impact of, 76; Reflection Points for, 77; resources for teaching, 77*b*; Story Maps with Character Perspectives (SMCP) strategy, 69; *The True Story of the Three Little Pigs* (Scieszka), 76

CHATTON, B., 113*b*, 143

CHERLAND, J., 62, 118, 141

CHILDREN'S BOOKS. *See* Books

CHILDREN'S CHOICES (INTERNATIONAL READING ASSOCIATION), 31

CHOCOLATE TOUCH, 92, 93*f*

CHOI, S.N., 32*b*, 145

CIVIL WAR: texts for discussions that relate to, 32, 32*b*

CLASSROOMS: author's, 28–36; descriptions of, 12–16; literature discussion groups in, 19–36

CLEARY, B., 31*b*, 145

COERR, E., 32*b*, 145

COMMEYRAS, M., 60, 141

CONTEXT CLUES, 79–80

CONVERSATION: "grand conversations," 5–6, 37, 65. *See also* Literature discussion(s)

CONVERSATIONAL DISCUSSION GROUPS (CDGS), 26–27

COONEY, C., 31*b*, 145; *The Face on the Milk Carton,* 57, 68, 85

COUSINS (HAMILTON), 125; discussions, 73–76, 84–85, 118, 121; example response log, 70–71

CRACKER JACKSON (BYARS), 48, 120–121; example observation notes, 106, 106*f;* example responses to, 47; student comments on, 117–118

CRITICAL LITERACY, 62–65; sources for teaching, 63*b*

CRITICAL QUESTIONS, 62–65; Reflection Points, 64; sources for teaching, 63*b*

CROW BOY (YASHIMA), 54–55, 83

CULTURAL INFLUENCES: on literature discussions, 114–135; Reflection Points for, 115

D

DANIELS, H., 25*b*, 142
DAVIES, B., 62, 142
dePAOLA, T., 84*b*, 145
DEWEY, J., 11, 142
DIALOGUE JOURNALS, 46, 46*b*
DISCUSSION(S). *See* Literature discussion(s)
DISCUSSION GROUPS. *See* Literature discussion groups
DISCUSSION LISTS, 38–42; example use of, 39–42; questions for, 42
DISHNER, E., 46*b*
DUGAN, J., 25*b*, 27–28, 142

E

EDELSKY, C., 62, 141
EEDS, M., 5–6, 37, 58, 142
EMERY, D., 69, 77*b*, 142
EVALUATION. *See* Assessment
EVANS, KAREN S., 122*b*, 123, 142; beliefs about reading instruction and literacy
    learning, 8–12; classrooms, 28–36; identity, 5–7

F

THE FACE ON THE MILK CARTON (COONEY), 68; example discussion, 57; student
    theme suggestions, 85
FAREST, C., 46*b*, 142
FARNAN, N., 43, 51*b*, 143
FICTION. *See* Books; Historical fiction
FISHER, P., 82*b*, 142
FITZGERALD, J., 68*b*, 69, 77*b*, 142
FLITTERMAN-KING, S., 44
FOX, P., 20, 145

G

GALDA, L., 29, 142
GALLAS, K., 122*b*, 142
GAMBRELL, L.B., 25*b*
GENDER INFLUENCES, 114–115; bossiness and, 132–134; "boy behavior," 123; ex-
    ample student discussion, 115–117; inequities in literature discussions
    and small-group contexts, 122*b*; multiple perspectives and, 117–119;
    preference for same-gender groups, 119–126; Reflection Points for,
    123–124, 126; student comments on, 117–118; student perceptions of,
    115–126; "us versus them" mentality, 116–117, 133
GETTING READY (LITERACY EVENT), 27
THE GIVER (LOWRY), 34
GOODBYE, CHICKEN LITTLE (BYARS), 85

GOODMAN, Y., 104, 142

GRADING, 110–113; vs assessment, 102–104; observations for, 110–113; Reflection Points for, 103–104

GRAND CONVERSATIONS, 5–6, 37, 65

THE GREAT GILLY HOPKINS (PATERSON), 39, 55, 116; example discussion, 63–64; example peer evaluation, 92, 94*f*; example response log entries, 56, 72–73; example SMCP strategy with, 70; example Story Maps with Character Perspectives sheet, 70, 71*f*

GROUP DISCUSSION(S). *See* Literature discussion(s)

GROUPS: "bossy people" and, 126–127; same-gender, 119–126, 134; small-group contexts, 122*b*

GUZZETTI, B., 122*b*, 142

H

HAMILTON, V., 145; *Cousins*, 70–71, 73–76, 84–85, 118, 121, 125

HANCOCK, M., 43, 51, 51*b*, 143

HARSTE, J.C., 46*b*, 143

HESS, K., 32*b*, 145

HIGHFIELD, K., 24, 25*b*, 26, 113*b*, 143

HISTORICAL FICTION: picture books for Civil War discussions, 32, 32*b*; young adult novels for World War II discussions, 32, 32*b*

HOESTLANDT, J., 32*b*, 145

HOFFMAN, J.V., 43, 51*b*, 143

HOFFMAN, M., 84*b*, 145

HOLUBEC, E., 129, 143

HOMECOMING (VOIGT), 60–61

HONESTY, 99–102

HOPKINS, D., 32*b*, 145

HOW TO GET FABULOUSLY RICH (ROCKWELL), 39, 119–120, 125

HYLLBERG, M., 7

I

IDEA LISTS, 38–42

IDOL, L., 77*b*, 143

INDEPENDENT STUDY: preparing discussion groups for, 35–36

INSTRUCTION: reading, 8–12; skills, 66–87; vocabulary, 78–82

INSTRUCTIONAL SCAFFOLDING, 37–65

INTERNATIONAL READING ASSOCIATION, 31

I-R-E DISCUSSION PATTERN, 127

"I WONDER" STATEMENTS, 53, 55; examples, 55; Reflection Points for, 56–57

J

JOHNSON, D., 129, 143

JOHNSON, R., 129, 143

JOURNALS: dialogue journals, 46, 46*b*; literature response logs, 43–53; questions for reflection, 4; Thinking on Paper (literacy event), 27
JULIE OF THE WOLVES (GEORGE), 68

K

KAUFFMAN, G., 89, 144
KELLY, P., 43, 51*b*, 143
KIDWATCHING, 104

L

LAZAN, M.B., 32*b*, 145
LEADERSHIP, 127–132; group discussions, 128, 130; Reflection Points for, 132
LEE, J., 82*b*, 141
LEWIS, J.P., 68*b*, 141
LITERACY, CRITICAL, 62–65, 63*b*
LITERACY ASSESSMENT SOURCES, 113*b*
LITERACY EVENTS, 27
LITERACY INDICATORS, 104, 105*f*; interpretation of data with, 107–108; observation grid of, 107–108, 109*f*; observations from, 110–113; Reflection Points for, 104–105
LITERACY LEARNING, 8–12; Reflection Points for, 12; student thoughts on, 10
LITERATURE DISCUSSION(S), 21–23, 66–87; Civil War-related, 32, 32*b*; examples, 39–42, 73–75, 84–85; gender inequities in, 122*b*; "grand conversations," 5–6, 37, 65; integrating skills instruction with, 66–87; I-R-E pattern, 127; Reflection Points for, 35; response logs as springboards for, 48–50; round-robin, 37–65; RQL2 strategy (Respond, Question, Listen, and Link) for, 28; scaffolding for, 37–65; social and cultural influences on, 114–135; structured minidiscussions, 29; student responses to, 21–23; teacher-led, 57–58; topics for, 38–42, 137; Transactional Literature Discussions (TLDs), 27–28; World War II-related, 32, 32*b*
LITERATURE DISCUSSION GROUPS, 24–28, 88–113; assessing, 88–113; Book Club, 24–26; books for use in, 31, 31*b*; in classroom, 19–36; Conversational Discussion Groups (CDGs), 26–27; implementing, 19–36; initiating, 29; preparing for independent study, 35–36; rationale for, 19–36; resources for organizing, 25*b*; student perspectives on, 21–24
LITERATURE RESPONSE LOGS, 43–53; resources for, 51*b*; suggestions for use, 45
LITERATURE STUDY RATINGS, 91–92
LLOYD, C., 6, 143
LOGAN, J., 82*b*, 144
LOGS. *See* Journals
LOOKING BACK (LITERACY EVENT), 27
LOWRY, L., 32*b*, 34, 145

M

Manzo, A., 82b, 143

Manzo, U., 82b, 143

Martinez, M.G., 25b, 43, 51b, 143–144

McConaughy, S.H., 77b, 143

McMahon, S.I., 24, 25b, 26, 113b, 143

Mihalevich, C., 77b, 142

Miller, C., 46b, 142

minidiscussions, 29. *See also* Literature discussion(s)

Mitchell-Pierce, K., 53, 55, 143

Moje, E., 122b, 143

Monkey Island (Fox), 52, 116–117; aesthetic reading of, 20; example responses to, 47

multiple perspectives, 117–119

Myers, W.D., 3, 145

N

Naylor, P.R., 31b, 145; *Shiloh*, 1–2, 47, 70, 71f

Nichols, W., 82b, 144

nonfiction: picture books for Civil War discussions, 32, 32b; young adult novels for World War II discussions, 32, 32b

notetaking: observation notes, 106, 106f, 107–108, 110

O

Observation Grids, 108–110, 140; example, 107–108, 109f; Reflection Points for, 110

observation notes, 107; example, 106, 106f; interpretation of, 107–108; Reflection Points for, 107, 110

observations, 110–113

O'Flahavan, J., 25b, 26, 143–144

On My Own questions, 53–54

P

Paley, V., 57, 143

Paradis, E., 113b, 143

Pardo, L.S., 24, 25b, 26, 113b, 143

Paterson, K., 31b, 145; *The Great Gilly Hopkins*, 39, 55, 63–64, 70, 71f, 92, 94f

peer assessments, 90–92; examples, 92, 93f; student comments on, 95, 98; student perceptions of, 96–99; student responses to, 96–99; Student Self- and Peer-Assessment Form, 139

peer evaluation, 88; examples, 92, 94f

Perl, L., 32b, 145

personal experiences: integration with text-based information, 84–85

Pettit, J., 32b, 145

PICTURE BOOKS: nonfiction and historical fiction texts for Civil War discussions, 32, 32*b*. *See also* Books
PIERCE, K., 25*b*, 144
PLOT. *See* Story structure
POLACCO, P., 32*b*, 145

Q

QARs. *See* Question-Answer-Relationships
QUESTION-ANSWER-RELATIONSHIPS (QARs), 53, 63; lesson description, 54–55
QUESTIONS, 53–65; critical, 62–65, 63*b*; genuine, 57–62; "I wonder" statements, 53, 55; On My Own, 53–54; for reflection, 4; Reflection Points for, 56–57, 62; Right There, 53–54; "teacher questions," 57–58; Think and Search, 53–54; types of, 53–54

R

RAPHAEL, T.E., 24, 25*b*, 26, 53, 113*b*, 143
RAYBURN, S., 29, 142
READ-ALOUD BOOKS, 79–80
READENCE, J.E., 46*b*, 143–144
READERS, 23–24
READING: aesthetic, 20–21; Sustained Silent Reading (SSR), 35
READING AND THINKING ALOUD (LITERACY EVENT), 27
READING INSTRUCTION, 8–12
READING PROGRAMS, 68*b*
REFLECTION: Looking Back (literacy event), 27–28
REFLECTION POINTS: for aesthetic reading, 21; for assessment, 102; for assessment vs grading, 103–104; for book selection, 33, 35; for critical questions, 64; for cultural influences, 115; for discussion lists, 42; for discussions, 35; for gender influences, 123–124, 126; for implementing literature discussion groups, 28; for journal reflection, 4; for leadership issues, 132; for literacy indicators, 104–105; for literacy instruction, 12; for literacy learning, 9–10; for literature response logs, 56–57; for observation grids, 110; for observation notes, 107, 110; for questions, 62; for reading instruction, 9–10; for response logs, 45; for skills instruction, 67–68, 87; for SMCP lessons, 77; for social influences, 115; for theme strategy lessons, 86; for unanswered questions, 134; for vocabulary instruction, 82
REISS, J., 32*b*, 145
REPORT CARDS, 110–113
RESOURCES: for balanced reading programs, 68*b*; for dialogue journals, 46*b*; to explore gender inequities, 122*b*; for literacy assessment, 113*b*; for literature response logs, 51*b*; for organizing discussion groups, 25*b*; for teaching critical questions and critical literacy, 63*b*; for teaching story structure

and character perspective/development, 77*b*; for vocabulary instruction, 82*b*

RESPONSE LOGS, 43–53; examples, 47–48, 72–73; resources for using, 51*b*; round-robin, 52–53; sample entries, 56; as springboards for discussion, 48–50; suggestions for use, 45; teacher response to, 51–52

RICHARDSON, V., 6, 144

RIGHT THERE QUESTIONS, 53–54

RINGOLD, F., 32*b*, 145

ROCKWELL, T., 31*b*, 146; *How to Get Fabulously Rich*, 39, 119–120, 125

ROSENBLATT, L., 10, 20, 144

ROSER, N.L., 25*b*, 43, 51*b*, 143–144

ROUND-ROBIN DISCUSSIONS, 37–65

ROUND-ROBIN RESPONSE LOGS, 52–53

ROUTMAN, R., 51*b*, 104, 112, 113*b*, 144

RQL2 STRATEGY (RESPOND, QUESTION, LISTEN, AND LINK), 28

RUPLEY, W., 82*b*, 144

RYLANT, C., 70, 146

S

SAME-GENDER GROUPS, 134; example discussion, 120–121s; preference for, 119–126

SCAFFOLDING, 37–65

SCIESZKA, J., 76, 146

SCORPIONS (MYERS), 3

SEBESTYEN, O., 146; *Words By Heart*, 47, 55, 69, 79, 83

SELF-ASSESSMENTS, 88, 90–92, 101–102; criteria for, 90–91, 91*t*; rating scale for, 90; student comments on, 98; student perceptions of, 96–99; student responses to, 96–99; Student Self- and Peer-Assessment Form, 139

SELF-EVALUATIONS. *See* Self-assessments

SELF-REFLECTION, 97, 101

SHANAHAN, S., 77*b*, 144

SHANAHAN, T., 77*b*, 144

SHARING SUSAN, 19, 30, 47–48, 58–59

SHEPARDSON, D., 122*b*, 143

SHILOH (NAYLOR): discussion vignette, 1–2; example responses to, 47; example SMCP strategy with, 70, 71*f*

SHORT, K.G., 25*b*, 46*b*, 89, 142, 144

SIMPSON, A., 62–63, 63*b*, 144

SKEPTICISM, 62

SKILLS INSTRUCTION: integrating with literature discussions, 66–87; Reflection Points for, 67–68, 87

SMALL-GROUP CONTEXTS, 122*b*

SMCP STRATEGY. *See* Story Maps with Character Perspectives strategy

SMITH, J., 82*b*, 142

SMITH, M., 113*b*, 143

Smith, R.K., 31*b*, 96, 146

social influences: on literature discussions, 114–135; Reflection Points for, 115

Spiegel, D.L., 68*b*, 69, 77*b*, 142

SSR. *See* Sustained Silent Reading

Staal, L., 77*b*, 144

Stanzi, L.C., 29, 142

Story Maps with Character Perspectives (SMCP) strategy, 69, 75–76, 138; examples, 70, 71*f*, 72*f*; Reflection Points for, 77

story structure, 68–77; Reflection Points for, 77; resources for teaching, 77*b*

Strider (Cleary), 47

structured minidiscussion, 29

student assessments: honesty in, 99–102; self-assessments, 88, 90–92, 96–99, 101–102; student comments on, 99–100; Student Self- and Peer-Assessment Form, 139

students: "bossy people," 115, 126–134; comments on student assessments, 99–100; literature study ratings for, 91–92; participation in book selection, 33; peer assessments, 92, 93*f*; peer evaluations, 92, 94*f*; perceptions of "bossy people," 126–134; perceptions of gender, 115–126; perceptions of self- and peer assessments, 96–99; perspectives on discussion groups, 21–24; preference for same-gender groups, 119–126; as readers, 23–24; responses to literature discussion, 21–23; responses to literature study evaluations, 98–99; role in assessment, 96–99; theme suggestions, 83, 85; thoughts on literacy learning, 10

Student Self- and Peer Assessment Form, 139

Sustained Silent Reading (SSR), 35

T

Talking (literacy event), 27

teacher assessment, 104–110

teacher-led discussion(s), 57–58

"teacher questions," 57–58

teachers: response to student response logs, 51–52

Teen magazine, 15

Temple, C., 63*b*, 144

theme, 82–87; children's books for strategy lessons on, 84*b*; Reflection Points for, 86; student suggestions, 83, 85

Think and Search questions, 53–54

Thinking on Paper (literacy event), 27

Tidwell, D., 6, 143

Tierney, R.J., 46*b*, 144

Tiger Beat magazine, 15

TLDs. *See* Transactional Literature Discussions

topic ideas, 38–42, 137

transaction, 10

Transactional Literature Discussions (TLDs), 27–28

THE TRUE STORY OF THE THREE LITTLE PIGS (SCIESZKA), 76
TUCK EVERLASTING (BABBITT), 29
TURNER, A., 32*b*, 146

V

VAN ALLSBURG, C., 84*b*, 146
VOCABULARY INSTRUCTION, 78–82; with read-aloud books, 79–80; Reflection
  Points for, 82; resources for, 82*b*
VOIGT, C., 60, 146
VYGOTSKY, L.S., 11, 52, 144

W

THE WAR WITH GRANDPA (SMITH), 96
WATSON, D., 113*b*, 144
WEAVER, C., 68*b*, 144
WELLS, D., 5–6, 37, 58, 142
WERCHADLO, B., 51*b*, 144
WHITIN, D., 62, 63*b*, 144
WHITIN, P., 62, 63*b*, 144
WIENCEK, J., 25*b*, 26, 144
WILLIAMS, K.A., 68*b*, 141
WILLIAMS, W., 122*b*, 142
WINTER, J., 32*b*, 146
WOLLMAN-BONILLA, J., 51*b*, 144
WONDERING ON PAPER (LITERACY EVENT), 27
WORDS BY HEART (SEBESTYEN), 47, 55, 69, 79, 83
WORLD WAR II: texts for discussions that relate to, 32, 32*b*
WRITING: literature response logs, 43–53; Thinking on Paper (literacy event), 27;
  Wondering on Paper (literacy event), 27

Y–Z

YASHIMA, T., 54–55, 83, 146
YOUNG ADULT NOVELS: for World War II discussions, 32, 32*b*. *See also* Books
YOVICH, S., 113*b*, 143
ZONE OF PROXIMAL DEVELOPMENT (ZPD), 11
ZPD. *See* Zone of Proximal Development